PASTORAL PRAYERS
THROUGH THE YEAR

Pastoral Prayers through the Year

AN ANTHOLOGY
BY CONTEMPORARY LEADERS
AND TEACHERS
OF AMERICAN PROTESTANTISM

COMPILED AND EDITED
WITH AN INTRODUCTION
by Robert L. Eddy

CHARLES SCRIBNER'S SONS | *New York*

1532141

CONTENTS

7

INTRODUCTION

I. OF PRAYER

PRAYER is the ascent of the soul to God. So taught Basil of Caesarea. Ancient saints and later mystics have declared they found it so. Devout and thoughtful men of our own time have felt the same way when they have described prayer as communion of the soul with the Spirit of God.

This communion of soul with Soul needs no words, for it is beyond words. An ardent admirer of St. Francis of Assisi once managed to lodge in a room next to St. Francis, in the hope of hearing prayers of matchless beauty. But all he heard at various times all night long were the saint's simple but impassioned cries, "My God!—My God!"

We who live down in the foothills of holy vision need for our prayers the clothing of words. Without words many of us might never be sure that our fleeting moments of religious feeling were not just lofty sentiments or high resolves. These will leave pleasant sensations, but not the trembling joy of having confronted that other, greater Being, nor the strength which follows that joy.

Words are the preparation and accompaniment for true prayer. Their source is the longing of the heart, the depths of a man's inner being, dredged up with all their earthy attachments. ("Father, if thou be willing, remove this cup from me.") But the feelings of the heart must be framed and aimed in words by the mind if the soul is to sense its fulfilment in prayer. Heart and mind go hand in hand; religious feeling calls for words, while the words themselves as they are uttered suggest other and deeper feelings, the more fervently they are spoken.

What really happens in prayer, that secret moment when, all un-watched, the soul opens its door before the Divine presence —this is an article of faith to our mere minds. We are able to live in the power of assurance we get from this kind of prayer, and we are not able to live so well without it. This is enough.

2. OF PRAYER IN WORSHIP

WORSHIP is a sustained rendering of praise and love to God. We may worship with our lives, but they must be guided, upheld, and driven by those hours of conscious word and song in which we seek His Face. The quest for God may be undertaken alone, but this way is hazardous, difficult, and pathetically unnecessary. Most men with an eye to the serious business of worship have agreed that much more is accomplished for each when two or three or more are gathered together in one place.

In the common, holy desire of men assembled to serve, to find, and to visit with the Divine Presence, prayer is the very language of the ensuing quest. Thus in a sense worship *is* prayer, and all its transactions breathe of that upper air. Thus rightly do the Episcopalians call their divine service "morning prayer." So great and so vital an event in a man's whole life finds place for singing, for offering, for instruction, even for announcements, but the business of the time is prayer. As a mood of holy desire it pervades the whole hour, and it breaks forth into many short articulations as invocation, collect, dedication, benediction, and such other prayers as the usages of the church or the minister call for.

In addition to these short prayers, which are the sustaining-posts of the people's reverent mood, many of the Protestant church services provide for one longer prayer by the pastor. This prayer is indeterminate in form and content; it is called variously the general prayer, the free prayer, or the morning prayer. It was once called "the long prayer." It is quite generally understood as the pastoral prayer.

3. OF THE PASTORAL PRAYER

IN ROMAN Catholic and Episcopal services the confirmed worshiper feels no need for a single long, general prayer by the priest. The whole service is in a sense a prayer. It embraces and sets forth by symbol or sentence all that prayer can say. It is a traditional vehicle in which each worshiper may let his own thanksgivings and petitions ride.

But to the other Protestants the prayers of former saints were not enough for their services of worship. They sought to acquaint themselves at first hand with the Deity, in Emerson's phrase. They were zealous to bring to God in prayer and worship their devotion and their several needs in words which sprang from their personal lives. They also believed devoutly in the importance of the individual, just as he really was, in the service of worship. And so they added to the several short prayers a longer prayer in which the minister strode through the formal structures of the service to give their people's own prayers for the particular day. With the Lutherans, the "general prayer," as they call it, is basically a pattern of freely chosen liturgical phrases, which the pastor may also employ to finish and gild his congregation's own thoughts as he offers them. This rather slight deviation from the Roman rite in church prayer finds its opposite pole in the pastoral prayers of the early American religious frontier, where homespun pastors offered, in all reverence, petitions so specific that they made up a chronicle of the news of the week. Here are some of the petitions of the Rev. Mr. Rozencrantz, a character in a novel, which the author conceives were offered at a Sunday church service in Oriskany, New York, in 1777:

"*God Almighty*, our *Heavenly Father*, we return thanks for the good lambing we have had this year, particularly Joe Bellinger, who has had eleven couples lambed from his twelve ewes, which is a record in this county.

"*O Almighty God*, we ask Thy compassion and aid for all of us who are in sickness. We ask it for Petey Paris, who got the flux real bad on Saturday. His Uncle Isaac Paris sent the news to us and asks our prayers and says that he has got in a new supply of calicos . . . some new hats . . . and grindstones . . .

"O God Almighty, our own Colonel Peter Bellinger wants the fourth company to muster at Dayton tomorrow . . .

"The muster will be at eight o'clock sharp on Monday morning.

"For Christ's sake, Amen." *

Between these extremes most of our Protestant churches have a place in their Sunday services for their ministers to say whatever is needed to make each service a fully-rounded presentation of the worshiper to God.

In view of the value of prayer and of freedom, it may be wondered that the pastoral prayer did not become the high point of the Protestant worship service, like the elevation of the host in the Catholic mass. But there are many reasons why it did not. First, the same forces which released the pastoral prayer from rigidity also enlarged that extraordinary growth, the Protestant sermon, which rightly or wrongly did become the high point, or area, of interest. Then, too, there is a limited number of thoughts which are sufficiently vital, all-embracing, and high to seem proper to such a prayer. The top of Mount Monadnock is no larger than the floor of a small room. At what might have been the high point of the service, the worshiper hears and needs and expects only a few thoughts, usually familiar.

Further, the pastoral prayer did not seize the high point of the Protestant worshipers' interest because it was not intended to be literally the minister's vicarious offering of his people's prayers, but rather to stake out in the service a "season of prayer," as it is sometimes called, in which worshipers are to concentrate on offering their own need and joy to their heavenly Father. In this "season," the minister's words at best only symbolize or suggest the people's thoughts. They may also suggest what thoughts

* From Walter D. Edmonds, *Drums Along the Mohawk*, Boston: Little, Brown & Company, pp. 156–158.

ought to be in their minds, but in no case are they to take the place of the individual's offerings. The minister's words in the Protestant general prayer are intended to serve only as background music to the true prayers all around him, rising mysteriously from the believers' thoughts which audible words have helped to inspire. Indeed, a pastoral prayer is "successful" when it does not call attention to itself, but rather to the holy Person of its address.

Lastly, the pastoral prayer failed to win and hold the high point of the Protestant service because it has everything to do with a mood of awareness of God which is a very tenuous, fleeting thing for any but mystics, and sometimes for them too. The wind blows where it wills, and the Spirit may elude a man all during the pastoral prayer, and touch him lightly at the benediction. Without the prayer, the benediction might have meant only, "Goodbye." And thus, as it should be, the pastoral prayer is content not to be the high point of the service so far as the worshiper knows.

Thus the pastoral prayer lives on in Protestant services, a sublime paradox, like life itself. It is longer than a collect, that all may enter the "season of prayer," yet it outlives its usefulness as soon as the dove of the Spirit has flown the room, which is often all too soon. It is a frontal attack on the task of talking to God, made in the knowledge (available, at least) that we meet Him and He meets us usually when we are just a little off guard. Yet the effort has not been all in vain. Without it the service would seem a little bleak even to the casual layman. With it, he may at least feel that the minister and he have tried to do their duty. "I reach the Eternal Goodness," wrote one western mystic, "not by trying, not without having tried." The day brightens, peace nears the man who has dropped everything to try to follow the pastoral prayer. Through the years it has shortened; in time ahead it does not seem likely to be given up.

MANY a man may wonder, however, what to look for in a pastoral prayer, just what its purpose is, and how it is put together. Ministers would like to be reassured that their pastoral prayer fulfills its purpose well, that theirs are the tools and spirit from which inspiring prayers are formed.

Where a prayer has missed fire the hearer may complain that it seemed long and rambling. Even with complete respect, perhaps he did not follow its course and make it his own prayer's course to the mutual Amen. This may be due to his own mental rambling, ill-schooled and unwilling really to follow his pastor, here, literally, a shepherd. Meanwhile his observation may have been right: maybe the prayer was long and rambling. The length could be due to the pastor's love of God, of tradition, and of duty to pray in full. The ramble would be the result of his feeling that his prayer needed no clearly visible organization; he would let the wind blow him where it willed, but not into any patterned utterance. Content that his prayer should be background music for the people's own prayers, he lets the outline of his own prayer recede to the vanishing point. When the pastor's path in prayer thus becomes a maze, it is not to be wondered if the people err and stray into desires and devices of their own hearts, their attention tossed off by the centrifugal force of the minister's wandering course in prayer.

But there have been ministers in the free churches, and we may hope and believe that there are more now, who make much of the pastoral prayer, and whose people are lifted by it. For them the prayers of the service are not preliminaries to the sermon, but are great ends in themselves. For them preparing their prayers takes the same kind of premeditation as readying the sermon does. Attractive to them is *A Book of Worship for Free Churches* (Oxford, 1948) whose very title would have been a startling contradiction in terms a century ago, to say nothing of three centuries ago. For them the pastoral prayer can be the soul's dedication of the mind's talents in making a work of art in words. To them it is always interesting to ask of the pastoral prayer, what are its author's requirements, what are its materials, its parts, manner, and tools?

The only requirements of the maker of pastoral prayers are that he have a religion of his own and that he have the power to convey it to others so that their awareness of God is sharpened. No prayers have any lifting power which have not come from a man's honest, first-hand walks with the Almighty. The best-stocked and most highly disciplined mind prepares its authentic prayers only on orders from a deep longing which cries for them. The man with only a vague knowledge about God which he keeps confusing with human ideals and other, lesser notions is apt to offer prayers of limited beauty and lifting power because even a highly skilled imagination and talent do not have the elemental power of God which the true believer can release from his own heart.

But the other requirement in making prayers is to communicate prayers, unless we are to "speak with tongues" for the rest of this Dispensation. The great Bible verses "carry alive into the heart" in Wordsworth's phrase, the religious sentiments, and it is very likely that these verses were carefully thought out before they were written down. The minister's prayers, in like manner, are caught and shaped with the painful toil of a loving artisan, bent on conveying them from his heart to those of his hearers. In addition to his own religion and sincerity he draws on all his other resources in offering the morning prayer. Genius is a little inspiration and much perspiration. The great prayers of Christendom received their authors' loving intent, their wit and skill and fervent voice before they became classic, showing the meaning in part of worshiping "with all thy heart, and soul, and strength, and mind." Surely no man would knowingly with-hold any talent he had in fashioning his and his people's prayers which would help lead them through the inward maze to the secret place of the Most High. As in any other work of art touching the soul of man, prayer has its materials, its forms, its manner, its tools, and its mode of conveyance to waiting fellow-men.

The *materials* of spoken prayer are its thoughts. And a minister's second thoughts as he readies his prayers are more likely later to convey his religion to his hearers than are his first. He needs thoughts to make his otherworldly visit with God mean-ingful to this world, its scenes, its men, its varied life. He needs thoughts that this meaningful visit may turn the power of prayer into vistas and resolves of life which lift it to a higher plane. He needs thought also, to keep the mind from wandering in prayer until it is no longer prayer. Thought in prayer brings to God all a man's great discoveries and convictions for His chastening or approval. But it takes more thought not to fall over into preaching to God, forgetting our ignorance when talking to Him at all.

The *form* of the pastoral prayer would be its size and its parts. It has become shorter in late years for many reasons. The fact that it probably seems longer to the hearer than it is surely is one reason. We have suggested others already, the demands for only the highest thoughts, the short span of a man's religious attention, but there are still others. One is the limitation imposed on the very vocabulary of prayer. It is said that Islam has ninety-nine words for Allah. But Christian prayer knows only three that are unmistakeable, universal names for the Deity: God, Father, and Lord. But the pastoral prayer finds its glory now in its very brevity. The history of the arts is full of stories telling how limitations enhanced creation rather than frustrating it. Shakespeare's sonnets in "their convent's narrow room" and Bach's frail clavichord both expressed the quintessence of all there was to say. Thus the pastoral prayer becomes short that it may be a prayer indeed.

The form of the pastoral prayer includes the number and shape of its parts. The various kinds of Christian prayer include adoration, thanksgiving, confession, intercession and petition. It is very unusual to find all five in the pastoral prayer. Brevity almost prohibits it, to begin with. Some parts have already been heard in the service, particularly the first, and, in the older churches, an office of confession has been rendered. Perhaps another reason may be that these five modes of prayer are so far apart in spirit and content that they cannot be welded either gracefully or even plausibly into one short address to the Lord. And if this fusion is attempted, one or more parts must shrink to a sentence or two if the others are to be a full expression of the minister's holy desires for the morning.

But the attempt to render a few short, pithy sentences of each type of prayer in one pastoral prayer does not seem unnatural either. This is particularly true if the prayer appears to be the one great chance to commune with God in the service, with the rest of the service seen as preparatory or resulting action.

Suppose a pastoral prayer to be like a very short visit between long absences from one's earthly father. This could begin with salutation and telling what the visit meant, corresponding to adoration. Then might come gratitude for paternal provision, for gifts sent (thanksgiving), and then, in the midst of all this joy, painful recollection that father is greater, older, and wiser, that his gifts have been partly neglected, partly wasted (confession). Then could come hopes that brothers and sisters would be kept from like faults and be continued the same gifts (intercession), and last of all, requests for all the things needful until the next visit, that only father can give or send (petition). Such a prayer, if carefully framed in taut, raw-boned mother-English, could hold the hearer and carry him with its design and movement without seeming longer than many another kind. Most pastoral prayers however have no more than two or three of the five varieties of intent in them. They may mingle and repeat the parts like the subjects in a symphonic poem.

On the practical side, however, when preparing a pastoral prayer, one sees how hard it is to try to use all five varieties in one prayer. Dean Sperry of Harvard once said, "A pastoral prayer cannot be an airplane flight over the whole field of religion." We can imagine how blurred an impression our people's minds would have of a "complete" or "total" prayer. A pastoral prayer may have only two or three parts so as to have impact, to stir the people without tiring them. But in preparing the whole service the minister is helped if he keeps in the back of his mind the whole gamut of the varieties of prayer.

The *manner* of the pastoral prayer, as has been strongly hinted already, is the manner of poetry. Prayer is like poetry at the point of definition: both are indefinable and unmistakeable, and the two are parallel to infinity. This fact is lost on us as result of the small number of those who have made a reputation in the writing of both prose prayers and general poetry. One thinks right away of John Donne, George Herbert, Samuel Johnson, Christina Rossetti, and Robert Louis Stevenson, but there are not many more. Yet how many of the canons of poetry are found in all the classic Christian prayers: economy and simplicity of words, symbolic and figurative projection of thoughts, the aforesaid "carrying alive into the heart" the *feelings* of the speaker about what is finally true—everything except meter in poetry is to be found in the manner of the pastoral prayer, in the ways in which the minister charges the "season of prayer" with that special quality which changes it from a time of address to God to a chance for a direct encounter with Him. And like the poet the maker of pulpit prayers must have an alert and musical ear.

The *tools* of the pastoral prayer are the words themselves, which in poetic manner form and shape the thoughts which rise from the minister's own life with God in the moment of his chance to pray aloud with and for his people. Beyond what has already been said about the words might be added a note about quotation. The pastoral prayer is a meeting of the ages with the moment; in it belong phrases from the past. These unite the hearers in fellowship with the cloud of witnesses around who first uttered them. The old words do again what they did before, and inspire the reciter to give his own thoughts and feelings better words. C. G. Montefiore has shown that the Lord's Prayer is a perfect gathering of phrases from synagogue prayers all commonly used in Christ's time. Christian prayer ever since has been in part an accumulating custody of the minted insights of the past. Just as good steel needs old iron as well as native ore in its making, so the great pastoral prayers have shown a deft and loving weaving of ancient scriptures, prayer, and liturgy with the authentic flashes of modern poetry and the sometimes rude but always dignified simplicity of what may be called only in a most limited sense one's own words. A minister may well wonder why he should rely wholly on his own clumsy tools when others which are not are stretched out to him and will do the job.

Last of all, *mode of conveyance* must be right if the pastoral prayer is to be a prayer indeed. The minister must have the hearers in mind from the beginning, and offer the prayer so that its sounds, as well as its thought and words, will move them to what is true prayer for them. This means, for the minister, knowing his people particularly and extensively. More important, it means knowing what they have in common. If Shakespeare's greatness lay in his power to make his characters speak as they would have spoken if they had been Shakespeare, so the minister in prayer must speak as his people would speak if they were he.

Delivery of the pastoral prayer requires, again, the same kind of premeditation used in getting its contents ready. The disciplines of a fine actor are required to save the most eloquent composition from drowning in a welter of stumbling, speed, strange pauses, monotone, the note of sadness which actually is the minister's seriousness (and often strangely sounding like boredom), or combinations of these, all very natural responses of a sincere man deep in prayer, yet strangling and killing the chances of the lay soul's ever getting to the door in him to the Spirit beyond. Thus a prayer written in tranquillity saves for the time of offering it all the energies of the minister's mind to insure best that it will stir and lift the hearts of the hearers because thus it has become their prayer too.

The great prayers would seem at first, like the poets, to be born, not made, but clothes must be added after birth. The great works of art cry innocent artlessness to the laity, who only get what the art reveals, seldom very much of the art itself. So the pastoral prayer, if it is to be in any sense a ladder of ascent for souls to God, must be with every native talent fitly framed together unto the temple of the Lord.

5. OF THIS BOOK OF PASTORAL PRAYERS

THIS collection comes from contemporary leaders and teachers of religion who have had more than ordinary concern for pulpit prayers as the thoughtful expressions of their own religion in this form. The work has enjoyed the sponsorship of the Congregational Commission on Evangelism. It has been built of contributions solicited from authors of books on prayer, from eminent preachers, from national religious leaders, from seminary professors in the field of worship and in other fields, and from representative pastors in many parts of the country who were recommended by the Evangelism Secretaries of their respective denominations.

The purpose of the book is primarily to lead men closer to God through the longer, pastoral prayers as they are already helped through the several excellent collections of shorter prayers. They are not merely to be read, they are to be prayed and lived in the reader's private life.

It is hoped that in addition the anthology may do something for the pastoral prayer. Being able to see it ought to enhance hearing it. The reader will remember that these are only the outer garments of the prayers proper. He must make allowance for the absence of familiar faces, especially that of his minister, the absence, too of the church building and the atmosphere and mood of the Sunday worshiper in church, all of which are indispensable parts of the pastoral prayer. But he will be able to see how it is put together, how the minister employs word and phrase to build the mood in which is sensed the closer presence of the Redeeming Spirit. Ministers and any others who may ever be called upon to offer prayer may find here both instruction and encouragement. The many men who feel that they are alone in laboring to prepare their pastoral prayers will here find that they are in a goodly fellowship. As the prayers are read (and prayed and lived) in the devotions of our ministers, we hope that they are helped on their way to lifting up the hearts of all our people.

My gratitude endures for the kindness of Dr. Wofford C. Timmons, late director of the Congregational Commission on Evangelism. It was he who urged me on in this work. He lent the sponsorship of the commission to this project, and showed warm and brotherly interest in it. I am also happy to express my gratitude to the Reverend Professor Robert S. Illingworth of the English Department of Clark University and pastor of the Congregational Church of Barre, Massachusetts, who in his twin role of scholar of the English language and practicing pastor of an authentic faith of his own, holds the twin critical powers for reviewing wisely and kindly both the matter and the manner of pastoral prayers. He has read the manuscript and has made helpful suggestions. And to all the contributors who for the readers' sakes alone labored to build this little book I give my lasting gratitude and a prayer of thanksgiving that such men live to empty all their great powers for us that His will be done and His Kingdom come.

Little Compton, Rhode Island
1 November, 1958

PASTORAL PRAYERS
THROUGH THE YEAR

FOR THE FIRST SUNDAY
OF THE YEAR

O THOU God and everlasting Father of all mankind, we join with all thy family in giving thee heartfelt thanks for the blessings of this life which thou hast bestowed upon us in the year that has passed. Thou art from everlasting to everlasting, but we are only for the day. Our lives flow on with the river of time, bringing to us the ever-changing days with all their varied experiences. We have been sustained unto this day by our faith in thee and in thy Son our Saviour, the ever-living Christ.

We are conscious of our shortcomings, for we have fallen below our own ideals, and we know thou hast found us lacking both in faith and in action. We have not failed thee by intention, but we are often indifferent, confused, and weak. But thou hast not forsaken us, for we feel thy correcting Spirit, and we would, O God, be more responsive to thy leadings. Forgive us, O Father, once again and take not thy holy spirit from us. Let us feel thy forgiveness and the refreshment of thy abiding presence.

Let us be courageous as we face a New Year. We believe it is thy will that we shall go forward, profiting by our mistakes and overcoming our fears and weaknesses, keeping ever in mind thy multiplied blessings of the past.

Help us to rise up as men of God and go forward in thy strength and guidance and grace. For this great blessing we pray most earnestly, realizing how far short all mankind has come in fashioning the kind of world thou wouldst have. Turn the minds and the wills of men to thee, that thy laws may be obeyed and thy Spirit rule, that thy kingdom may fully come. May this new year be truly a new year for us. Make us new men and women through Christ; may our faith be stronger, our love of thee more pure, our obedience to thy law and to thy free spirit more perfect, and grant that in humility and continued perseverance we may serve thee and all thy needy children through all the days that thou dost grant us. And when dark days come, as come they will, may we look more perfectly to thee for the courage to carry on, knowing that thou wilt never forsake us. Guide us always, we pray, in the name of Jesus Christ our Lord and Saviour. *Amen.*

FREDERICK L. FAGLEY, *Late Secretary Emeritus, the General Council of Congregational Christian Churches*

FOR EPIPHANY

or THE SECOND SUNDAY IN JANUARY

ALMIGHTY God, loving Father, whose merciful care is over all thy works, in all places, among all the children of men; We come before thee this day as into the presence of the most holy. Quiet our thoughts, we pray thee, until in the stillness of this sacred hour we become more aware of thy presence. Help us, by thy spirit, to feel thee near us; to listen to the fatherly persuasion of thy voice; to open the doors of our hearts to thy guiding. Thou art always more ready to hear than we to speak, and more ready to give than we to ask. Hear us, then, O Father.

Lo! We have brought to thy house our weariness from the labor of the past week; our dreams and disappointments; our perplexities over what is right and what is wrong; our sorrows. We have brought also our joys, our satisfactions, our eager anticipations, and our thankfulness for thy goodness. All of these, good or bad, wise or foolish, we lift up to thee.

May thy goodness shine upon them, thy divine patience hold them in thy hand with understanding love, according to thy nature. Purge out of them, we pray thee, whatever is cheap or insincere or cowardly or self-centered. Cleanse the very thoughts of our hearts. Show us how we look, dear Lord, when seen in the light of thy being and thy beauty.

As thou didst reveal thyself in Christ to all the world at the first Epiphany, spreading the light of thine eternal love through his birth and life and death and resurrection, so come now to us, his disciples, in power and in peace and in fellowship. Come in power, and break the chains of those sins which enslave us; come in peace, and still the fevers which betray our sickening fears; come in thy Spirit of brotherhood which builds harmony and trust and mutual loyalty among men.

Not for ourselves alone do we pray, thou Companion and Lover of men. Help us to make our lives channels of blessing and helpfulness to all in need: to those who are near and familiar, whose deeper needs we often overlook; to those in distant places whom we forget; to all who desire or need our prayers; to any whom we may have hurt, or who have hurt us. Draw us together with the strong cords of thy tenderness and understanding. As we forgive those who have injured us, do thou, in thy great goodness, forgive both them and us, for without thee nothing is strong, nothing is holy.

Bless the nation to which we belong; bless it, and make it pure, and give us dedication to the highest and a sound public mind. Bless all nations, all peoples and races, and tongues, uniting them in the kingdom of thy Christ. Thou seest, O God, how fervently our leaders look for help: our statesmen and diplomats; our teachers and writers; our scientists and our artists; and all who use the spoken word to influence thought. Touch them, O Lord, and make them look to thee, from whom alone cometh salvation.

Finally, grant we pray thee that when we leave this house to return to our homes and our work, we may not leave thy presence, but may carry in our hearts through the week the knowledge of thy continuing presence, and the peace which thou alone canst give; through Jesus Christ our Lord, who with thee and the Holy Spirit liveth and reigneth one God, world without end. *Amen.*

John W. Suter, *Custodian of
the* Book of Common Prayer

FOR THE EPIPHANY SEASON

or THE THIRD SUNDAY IN JANUARY

Most holy and gracious God, who art Lord of the spirits of all mankind, and whose love embraces every human creature, in this hour of worship we praise and bless Thee for the manifestation to all the world of Thy dear and glorious Son, Christ Jesus. We thank Thee for the inestimable benefit given to the children of men in his coming into the world. Grant, we earnestly pray, that the day may soon come when all the kingdoms of this world shall become his kingdom, when before him, as before Thee, every knee shall bow.

Lord of the nations, before whom our kings and prime ministers and presidents are as little children, be pleased, we pray of Thine infinite mercy, to use us all as messengers of Thy truth. In Holy Writ Thou dost show us Thy righteous will that not one of Thy little ones should perish for lack of knowledge of that truth. Send us out in Thy name unto the last and the least of the lost. Give us the will to go bravely about this Thy business, laying aside the weight of worldly concerns, that our Redeemer's name may be spread abroad to the farthest bounds of the earth.

Quicken our understanding of his gospel of brotherhood, that we may know all men to be Thy children, as precious in Thy sight as we like to think ourselves. Grant that we may long for their prosperity in soul and in circumstance as we do for our own. Make us generous of our substance, our service and our prayers, to minister to every sort of spiritual and material need, among ourselves or in far lands. Keep us from the sin of false pride, whether of race or color, wealth or nation, since all of right stand erect before Thee as full brethren. As Christ our Lord came to one nation and people, yet became saviour and redeemer of all, so enlarge our vision to perceive that the mission of Thy gospel is one, not alone to east or west, north or south.

Among the peoples whom Thou wouldst redeem prosper, we beseech Thee, the cause of brotherhood and peace. Grant that by our patience, tolerance and forbearance, as well as by our holy zeal, we of Thy Church may be worthy instruments of him whom the Magi of old sought and found in Bethlehem, who came to our world as Prince of Peace. Forbid that we should erect into idols the lesser gods of our several nationalisms; silence upon our tongues the cries of race and clan. In all ways, may we who are strong strive never to exploit or to conquer, but to share and to serve.

These things we humbly ask, that our Lord Christ's way may be known upon earth and Thy saving health among all nations. *Amen.*

ELMER S. FREEMAN, *Sometime Secretary,*
The Congregational Commission on Evangelism
Pastor, The First Congregational Church, Montevideo, Minnesota

O GOD our Father, we come to Thee again to praise and glorify Thee, to confess our sin before Thee, to seek Thy forgiveness and Thy strength. Thou art our rock and our salvation; in Thee alone is our peace.

We bless Thee, O God, for the bounty and the beauty of the good earth that surrounds and sustains us, for the blessings of homes and families and friends, for health and vigor and work to do, for a free land in which to dwell. Truly Thou hast given us a goodly heritage, and our lines have fallen in pleasant places. We acknowledge with gratitude before Thee every good gift from Thy hand. But above all, we bless Thee for our greatest boon, Thy greatest gift, our Lord Jesus Christ. In Him Thou hast visited and redeemed Thy people, and our hearts overflow with a gratitude that cannot be spoken.

Save us, O Lord, not only from thanklessness before these gifts of Thine, but from disobedience to Thy holy will. In Jesus Thou hast shown us the way; too often we have forsaken it. Too often we have followed our own desires in forgetfulness of Thine. Not in gross and conscious sinning have we so often affronted Thee as in yielding to the subtler temptations of indifference and self-will. Forbid, O Lord, that our sense of righteousness should become a cloak to cover our awareness of disobedience, for we know that what we hide from ourselves we cannot hide from Thee. Strip away our masks that we may see ourselves as Thou seest us. Then by Thy mercy purge us of our selfishness, our callousness, our complacent deafness to Thy call.

We pray Thee, O God, as Thou hast bidden us to pray, for daily bread. Give us what we need, that we may provide for ourselves and for those we love. But let us not seek riches in indifference to the plight of those many millions of

Thy children who in poverty and hunger lack daily bread. Stir in us a deeper compassion, and show us how best to help them.

We pray for Thy forgiveness, as our Lord taught us. But let us never forget that its cost to us is a willingness to forgive. If we have injured any, help us to make amends; if any have injured us, help us to put away rancor and the spirit of ill will. Guard us from self-pity, and make us ministers of Thy reconciling love. *1532141*

What we ask in our relations with those about us we ask for the world of nations. Give peace in our time, O Lord, for it is Thou only that makest us to dwell in safety. We would seek peace by Thy ways, and not by the deceptive and uneasy ways of war or threat of war. Give wisdom to the leaders of the nations, and give to us all a steadfast will to think those thoughts and to do those things that make for peace.

We pray Thee, O God, to deliver us from evil. We do not ask for easy lives or for the cessation of all pain. As Thy blessed Son has led us in the way of the Cross, so let us follow Him. But as He has opened to us the way of deliverance from evil, so make us Thy servants that many may enter it. We would be His witness—in the house of God, in our homes, in our places of daily toil, in our communities and as Thou dost enable us, through all Thy world.

So let our lives be used by Thee, O God, for the advancement of Thy Kingdom. What we have of time or talent or words or substance we place before Thee; take Thou our selves and use us as Thou wilt. And Thine shall be the Kingdom, and the power, and the glory forever. *Amen.*

GEORGIA HARKNESS, *The Pacific School of Religion, Berkeley, California*

O LORD, our God, who is like unto Thee in all this universe? Thou who watchest over us in our downsitting and our uprising, in our goings and in our comings; Thou who hast ordained that man shall be a little lower than the angels; Thou who hast looked upon the creation of humankind and hast called it good; we come into Thy presence this morning, desiring that we may know Thy will. Content are we if we may hear Thy voice coming to us through some hymn, some word of Scripture, some word which shall be spoken by Thy servant. Delighted are we if we can find the finger of divinity stirring in our conscious life, pointing out to us where we have made our errors. But more thankful are we, our Father, if Thou wilt point to us the way to life and light.

We do not deserve Thy favor, nor yet Thy mercy. Yet because Thou has created us and dost love us with an immeasurable love, Thou wilt not leave us nor forsake us. In our moments of fear and discouragement, Thou art by our side. When we find ourselves in the valley of the shadow of death, there Thou dost stand to encompass us with Thine eternal love. When all about us is darkness and dread there cast against the vacuum of our darkness the light of Thy love and the glory of Thy radiance.

How can we but praise Thee when we attempt to fathom that which Thou hast done for us? How dare we neglect Thee when through all generations Thou has continued with us? We thank Thee the Father of all generations for the many blessings Thou hast bestowed upon each of us. In no measure do we deserve what Thou hast done for us and so many times are we neglectful in return for what Thou hast done.

We come confessing before Thee this morning, our thoughtlessness, our selfishness, our indifference. All these sins Thou knowest well for they have been a part of humanity from the very beginning and so we come seeking Thy forgiveness. Put the radiance of Thy Holy Spirit upon us that we may turn our back upon all those sins of self love; that we may leave the pathway of pride; that we may stop our avarice and malice; that we may be wholly Thy children in the attempt to be what Thou dost desire Thy children to be.

We dedicate ourselves anew, Our Heavenly Father, to the purpose of living the way of Christ as the only way of peace.

And so we come before Thy throne of grace this morning, O Thou who canst call us each by our name, who art never too busy to be directly concerned with what we are doing, to be pained when we falter, to be over-joyed when we stand up like men and acquit ourselves rightfully before others and before Thee. As we stand in Thy presence at this time, speak to us that we may hear Thy voice. Through Jesus Christ our Lord we pray. *Amen.*

GEORGE E. PARKINSON, *First Presbyterian Church, Canton, Ohio*

FOR THE FIRST SUNDAY IN FEBRUARY

ETERNAL God, Merciful Father, the source of what we are and the end of all that we may become, in the quietness of Thy House we join our hearts and voices in a moment of prayer. We thank Thee that Thou hast guided our feet to this place today. May we depart refreshed in soul and with a new peace and gladness in our spirits.

Thou hast provided us and all men with things beyond our
deserving.
Thou hast given to us life itself and minds and wills with
which to live.
Above all Thou hast given Thyself in Christ Jesus, the
Savior.
For all these things we do most humbly offer thanks and
praise.

At the same time we bow in Thy presence seeking forgiveness. We come confessing our failures and sinfulness. Thou
knowest the good which we neglect. Thou seest that alluring
evil seems to satisfy us. Cleanse us; and even as Thy Son declared forgiveness from His Cross, forgive us.

Gracious Father, Who art the Light of the world and of
every life, lighten our paths, we pray. Relying on our own
sense of direction, we stray far from righteousness and truth.
Lost in the darkness of self, we are useless to Thee. Help us to
live within Thy light. May we never depart from it.

O Living Spirit, Thou seest to the innermost parts of every
life. Thou knowest our hopes and aspirations. Keep them true,
we pray, to Thy cause. Breathe upon us to purify our motives
and to sanctify our chosen goals. Thou knowest too our doubts
and fears, our worries, our cares and anxieties. Grant us assurant
faith and brave conviction that we may rise above them to become fit servants in Thy Kingdom.

But we pray not alone for ourselves, selfishly. We commend
to Thy care
the sick and the suffering,
the bereaved and the sorrowing,
the bitter,
the disappointed and downhearted and disillusioned,
those stricken by tragedy,
and those who feel hopeless, having lost life's savor.

As it be within Thy will,
    heal them,
    comfort them in their distress,
    relieve and strengthen them in body, mind and spirit.

For all in positions of authority, for those in places of public trust in our own and in all lands, we pray. As they take counsel, grant them Thy Spirit of wisdom. As they work with their fellowmen, fill them with the spirit of love and mercy. Remind them and us, that this is Thy world and not ours, that Thy rules must govern our actions, that Thy will must become the natural end of all that we do.

With the same concern we lift before Thee all those who have not yet made life's great decision. As they persist in walking away from Thy Cross, turn them about. Save them from themselves. And inspire us, we pray, to influence them with an increasingly clear proclamation of the saving Gospel and with transparent lives through which Thou canst be seen. By Thy grace may we become the means by which Thy truth may be known to all men.

For Thy Church around the world we offer our prayers. For all who live in the Name of Christ, we lift our supplications. Guard and protect them from the forces which are not Thine. Lead them to courageous witness in word and deed. Keep them steadfast in the finest of Christ-like living. And let us never forget that wherever they may be, we belong to them and they to us, because we all belong to Thee.

These and all other things that we ought to pray, the personal petitions of every soul present here, we include in the words of our Lord Jesus Christ, as we pray in His name . . .

(Here the congregation joins with the minister in saying the Lord's Prayer.)

ARNOLD F. KELLER, *St. John's Lutheran Church, Allentown, Pennsylvania*

FOR THE SECOND SUNDAY
IN FEBRUARY

or for *THE SUNDAY BEFORE LINCOLN'S*
BIRTHDAY

INTERRACIAL SUNDAY

BROTHERHOOD SUNDAY

ETERNAL God our Judge and Redeemer, who of thy righteousness dost raise up prophets to demand justice, and of thy mercy dost bring forth shepherds of compassion, we praise thee for thy work of redemption among men in every age. To an errant Israel thou didst give both rebuke and a new promise. Thou didst break the bonds of Egypt. By the rivers of Babylon thou didst hear the lament of thy people. In the fulness of time thine own Son entered into the turmoil and suffering of our earthly realm. For all these marvelous works of righteousness and reconciliation, and for the servants and statesmen of thy kingdom in every generation, we praise thy name.

Look down, we pray, with pity on our own restlessness and fear-filled time. Thou knowest the hatreds that divide us from thy children of other races and classes and nations, the selfishness that hardens our hearts against hungry multitudes in many lands, the violence that shatters peace among the nations. From the dark of our souls we cry unto thee; from the dark of our age we turn to thy light.

Commission and enspirit us to meet the perils and possibilities of our time humbly and courageously, as thy servants and faithful messengers. Let us never rest content while men know hunger on a bountiful earth, or fear in a world of which thou art stay, or war in a community where all men are thy sons. Deliver us from insulating privilege that obscures the needs of humanity; from pride that scorns to do the servant's task; from poverty of faith that does not know thy will for us and our times. Use us as thy ministers of restoration to those who are broken in body or spirit, as thy messengers of hope to those from whom hope has gone, as thy prophets of justice to those who are oppressed and neglected.

In and beyond all our striving we turn again to thee, imploring thy forgiveness and invoking thy mighty power. From the travail of the world we pray that thou wilt bring a new day of justice and peace. Let the world know that thou art still the Omnipotent One. Make the mighty tremble and the wicked forsake their ways; with thy thunder fill our skies and drown the roar of our destroying weapons. Make clear thy kingdom among us, and in our time of stress establish thy reign supreme, through Jesus Christ our Lord. *Amen.*

LISTON POPE, *Dean of Yale Divinity School, New Haven, Connecticut*

FOR A THIRD SUNDAY IN FEBRUARY

or A SUNDAY IN LENT

O LORD our God, Who hast promised that in all places where Thou dost record Thy name Thou wilt meet with Thy people to bless them; behold our spirits which, eagerly and penitently we lay upon Thine altar. Here is our store of fears, hopes and ambitions; here is our accumulation of doubts, uncertainties and decisions which make up our lives. And here too we present our inmost selves—where good and evil, the petty and the great, are so intricately mingled. Enlighten our darkness, purge us of our weakness, shame us out of our arrogance and pride, and replenish the secret springs of our being with the water of life.

O God, Who art the Light of all those that put their steady trust in Thee—touch our eyes with clearness and place the world before them truly, that we may see through its illusions and never trust ourselves to it without the shield of faith and the sword of the spirit. In times of doubt and questioning when our faith is perplexed and when our belief is strained, give us the boldness to examine all truth; give us the insight to master all pretense; and give us the stability to hold fast all the sources of our strength.

O God, our gracious Father, Who hast warned us that Thou wilt require much of those to whom much is given, let Thy blessing rest upon all the work we sincerely attempt to do in Thy name, especially in the task of sharing Thy Word and winning souls to Thy service. Grant us so sure a confidence in Thy unfailing love that we may freely and joyously come to Thee whenever we are perplexed and discouraged, to be raised by Thee into that serener faith in which all sorrows are healed and all sins forgiven; into that diviner love which renders our service a joy and perfect freedom; and into that abiding peace which the world can neither give nor take away.

O God, Who alone canst uphold the minds of men; without whose beauty and goodness our souls are unfed; without whose truthfulness our reasons wither; forgive, we pray Thee, the blindness of our hearts, and in Thy mercy lead us out of our wanderings into Thy holy light. Though our bed be a stone, and though there be no ladder to lift our dream, yet shall we seek Thee because Thou first seekest us. Consecrate our lives to Thy will, giving us such clarity of mind, such purity of heart, such depth of faith, and such steadfastness of purpose, that, in Thy good time, we may come to think Thy thoughts after Thee.

Hear our prayer, O merciful God, for all whom our hearts remember; for the lonely and troubled of soul, for those tried by temptation or baffled by difficulty, for those sick in body and for those for whom the light of life has gone out in the darkness of death. Endue them and us with a strength to bear our burdens, a courage to walk undismayed, and a patience to wait the full revelation of Thy will. We pray it in the name of Jesus Christ, Thy Son, our Lord—to Whom be honor, praise and thanksgiving forever and ever. *Amen.*

ROBERT D. HERSHEY, *The Evangelical Lutheran Church of the Holy Trinity in New York*

FOR A NON-LENTEN SUNDAY IN FEBRUARY

O LIVING God, as we come into Thy presence this morning, we are deeply awed by Thy constancy, Thy quiet patience, Thy reticence, Thy hiddenness, the unfathomed and unfathomable abyss of Thy inscrutable being. We bow down before the historic disclosure of Thy heart in Jesus Christ who lived in our world and in a distinct and measurable period of time and in an identifiable patch of this earth.

But this morning, O life of our lives, our hearts are swept by a vast surge of thankfulness for Thy living touch on our souls here and now, in this very moment; for this Pentecost of quickening that can move in the very ground of our souls; for the cutting away of the graveclothes of sin and self-serving; for the raising us up from spiritual death; for setting our souls all atremble with the joy that in me, even me, the God of my Lord Jesus Christ lives and moves and draws me into being and sets me all afresh about His business.

O Friend of our souls, our truest Friend, how can we bear the joy of knowing that Thou art alive in our very hearts this day: revealing, guiding, healing, inclining, accenting; restraining, cauterizing, renewing, relating, reshaping. O living Guest of our lives, O Host in whose hands we were and are and will forever be, we praise and glorify Thee this day, that we can be wakened to Thy burning current of love and feel what it means to be touched by the power of Thy Holy Spirit.

O God of life, batter the doors of those who know Thee not. Roll away the stones. Pierce through every barrier and arouse them to the last joy, which until now they have been denied.

For our loved ones, for those in pain of mind or body, for those in church and state who keep together the outward house in which we live, we ask an especial outpouring of Thy compassion, Thy love, Thy healing, and Thy guiding light.

O living Lord, lay on this company such a burst of inner joy and compassion and mercy that they may sense the burden of the world's suffering and be vigilant under Thy leading in ministering to its healing. These things we ask in the name of the Risen Lord. *Amen.*

Douglas V. Steere, *Haverford College, Haverford, Pennsylvania*

FOR THE FIRST SUNDAY IN LENT

Almighty and everlasting God, we gather here to praise thy name. We have gladly put away the many labors or delights which would call us. We have overcome with zeal whatever may have stood between us and thy house that we might in this holy hour seek thy spirit. We laud and magnify thee as the builder of our world and all we know, our maker, defender, redeemer and friend. Deliver us, we pray from the veils before our eyes which dim our sight of thee. Grant that we may sense thy presence more keenly, that we may feel our imperfections more sorrowfully and learn of thy forgiveness more joyfully.

We thank thee for the blessings and abundance with which thou hast crowned our days.

For the provisions which thou hast made for our bodies and our homes by which we have sustained the long winter secure as thy sons and daughters,

We give thee thanks and praise, O Lord.

For the life we lead in this quiet and untroubled village, abounding in chances to serve one another, to bear one another's burdens, to weep with those who weep and rejoice with those who rejoice,

We give thee thanks and praise, O Lord.

For this blessed season of Lent, wherein we re-live with Christ those forty days of temptation and mortal trial, looking to the true purpose of the life of man found in giving his life back to thee in service and devotion,

We give thee thanks and praise, O Lord.

For the quiet hours of study and prayer now before us, for the sharing of our goods with the poor and of our time in worship services with our sister churches, for all that this may do to bring us nearer to the likeness of Jesus Christ,

We give thee thanks and praise, O Lord.

For the blessings of adversity, for hardship, even pain, for the temptation to despair, that in these shadows of our earthly valley we may come across the footsteps of the Master, who knew every trial, disappointment, and heartbreak, and yet who by his complete dedication to thee found power to overcome them all to the glory of thy holy name,

We give thee thanks and praise and dominion and power over us and our world, both now and for evermore.

We ask at Lent's beginning that thou forgive our *sins*.* O most mighty God and merciful Father who hast compassion upon all men, and who wouldest not the death of a sinner but rather that he should turn from his sin and be saved; Mercifully forgive us our trespasses; receive and comfort us who are grieved and wearied with the burden of our sins. Thy property is always to have mercy; to thee only it appertaineth to forgive sins. Spare us therefore, good Lord, spare thy people, whom thou hast redeemed; enter not into judgment with thy servants, but so turn thine anger from us and make us truly repent our faults, and so make haste to help us in this world that we may ever live with thee in the world to come, through Jesus Christ, our Lord.

For thy promise of *forgiveness* and deliverance of sin which thou hast made to all searching, humble hearts we give thee of our hearts' deep joy. And we would that the goodness of this hour rest upon all thy children. Bind us closer to all Christians in every tongue and climate. Lead our country and inspire its leaders. Be with the sick and distressed of body or mind that out of their depths they may find in thee the way unto life indeed.

And now before too soon we leave these holy walls we bring thee our *needs* for the week to come. Vouchsafe to continue unto us our portion of bread and of shelter. Save those we love from harm, nor let them fall into any kind of danger.

Grant us thy *strength* in the days ahead. Let us each take up his cross and follow thy son. Let us abandon self in seeking him in prayer and sacrifice. As we contend with the world, the flesh, and the devil, let the power of thine indwelling spirit work for us, fight for us, and speak for us unto the dawn of victory.

Lastly grant us thy *peace*. We pray not for the peace of idle-

* The Confession is a part of the Penitential Office for Ash Wednesday in the Episcopal *Book of Common Prayer*.

ness but that thy will may be our peace, wherever it leads us. We pray that our minds may be at peace with our hearts, our ideals at peace with our memories, thy voice at peace with our voice. Be with us all the week long, hear us when we pray, and bring us safe at the close of day to thy mansions above. This our morning prayer we have asked in the name and for the sake of Jesus Christ our Lord. *Amen.*

Robert L. Eddy, *United Congregational Church, Little Compton, Rhode Island*

FOR THE SECOND SUNDAY IN LENT

Unto Thee, our Father, who dost manifest Thy Grace in the unfailing succession of the seasons, we Thy children give Thee most humble and hearty thanks for these days so rich in meanings and memories. We bless Thee for the comradeships seen and unseen which attend our discipleship and illumine our worship.

We pray Thee especially this morning for an always deepening sense of the significance of the season as it summons us anew to confession, repentance, and consecration. Deliver us, we beseech Thee, from vain and froward worship. Forbid that through any pride we veil the full acknowledgment of hidden faults, and cleanse us from secret sins. In Thy mercy forgive us our faults of omission and commission in our ways and works, and empower us with a true and effective spirit of self-denial.

Grant that our repentance may go deeper than any foregoing of ease and self-indulgence, but may carry in it transformed loyalty, chastened obedience, and a full devotion to the Way, the Truth, and the Life of Jesus Christ, our Lord and

Master. May our fellowship with Him be continually enriched with reality and power. Grant that with the lengthening days we may be blessed with a keen vision of the business of the spirit and inform us with a kindling sense of the beauty of holiness.

If it be so that the roads of life we are asked to use should lead us to bear the weight of any cross, give us courage to take it up and grace so to bear it that we may victoriously fulfill in our Christian discipleship the Master's summons that those who would come after him must take up the cross and follow him. If we can not see far or clearly on the road ahead of us, may we trust his guiding love and wisdom, assured that so guided we cannot go astray.

Remember, we beseech Thee, all those with whom we make this Lenten pilgrimage of love and faith, and establish among us a Christian comradeship which knows no barriers of race or station.

We remember before Thee the weary and the overborne; grant Thy comfort and healing to any especially distressed in mind, body, or estate. May we ourselves become Thy ministers in their need.

Remember Thy troubled world and increase amongst us a wisdom to open its closed doors and end its dissensions. Teach us the secret of peace, and bless and extend our longings for such a fellowship as may add to the cross of Jesus his coronation. Bless and extend all our right ways with one another. Give us such opening and questing minds that we may in the days which lie ahead discover more clearly and follow more faithfully the deeper meaning of self-denial and sacrifice. And so may the season be blessed in fellowship, enriched in its spiritual power, and touched with the beauty of the enduring.

In His name, whom we seek to follow, *Amen.*

GAIUS GLENN ATKINS, Late Secretary of Evangelism in the Congregational Christian Churches

O HEAVENLY Father, we come. We come stooped and weary from all of the luggage with which we seem determined to travel: our claimful selves; our restless longing to be in different places than we are; to be doing different things than we are; to be different persons than we are: different wives and husbands, different parents, different children, different neighbors than we are. Yet although we stagger with these painful weights we carry, nevertheless we come.

O Father of mercy, do not turn us away or ask us of our own weak wills to lay these cumbers down. Weary and laden though we be, O let us come and bring these cares, all of them, for they are a part of us that we must confess openly before Thee.

O Father of each burdened soul, lift the drooping lids of our inward eyes that we may see Thee, and seeing Thee, that we may know these crushing burdens for what they are: blindness to the needs and possibilities of living and serving in the places where we stand, in the work to which we have already put our hands. Give us a vision of what it would mean not to do different things in a different place, but to do all that we do differently, or give us a clear leading to the next step and a willingness to accept the risks involved in taking it.

Open the inward eyes of our souls, O Lord, that we may recognize that the longing to be other than we are as husband, as wife, as parent, as son, as daughter is an authentic response to Thine own prior drawing. Make us able to see that the lack of faith, the grim fatalism about our own mediocrity of soul, about our own inability to change is a leaden collar of our own contriving. O strike off this heavy collar of spiritual discouragement, of hopelessness with ourselves, from the necks of those in this company who wear it. Grant to each one of us Thy forgiveness for not long ago accepting Thy forgiveness. And

49

with the lightened hearts of those who have been set gloriously free, send us gaily and joyfully from this place this very day to proclaim that we have met the living God, that He has struck off our burdens, that He has healed and warmed and made our scarred hearts to dance, and has sent us out to witness to His joy and power.

O God send us back to our families, back to our benches, back to our colleagues and neighbors lightened of heart and bold of spirit.

These things we ask in the name of One who makes yokes easy, burdens light, and out of whose abundance we take hope: in the name of Jesus Christ. *Amen.*

Douglas V. Steere, *Haverford College,*
Haverford, Pennsylvania

FOR THE FOURTH SUNDAY IN LENT

O Thou who hast preserved us to this hour and hast led our feet once more to Thy house, who hast called us who love Thee to rejoice together in Thy goodness, we remember that age after age the living have waited upon Thee and have found that of Thy faithfulness there is no end. As Thou wast with our fathers, so be Thou now to us a shelter by the way and a defense from every danger which can hurt the soul; open to us, we pray Thee, the fountains of Thy grace that we, being renewed, may live to the hurt of none, to the helping of many, and to Thy glory.

We recall that our Lord's face was steadfastly set to do Thy will, that he was continually strengthened by Thy presence and that he turned aside, even as he drew near to the city of his death, to lay hold upon that life which, coming from Thee, is eternal in Thee. So may we, as in reverent remembrance we celebrate his courage which drew not back from the cross, be renewed in our life. May we be greatened in our desire to serve Thee and may we discover anew that Thou withholdest from those who truly love Thee no needed thing.

As he broke the bread of life for his disciples and multiplied food abundantly for the great company of those who were weary and in need, so may Thy Holy Word ever be broken and multiplied to our understanding. So open our hearts and so order our minds that it may be to us as the bread of life and as living water for our souls. May we, being sustained by Thee in our pilgrimage, neither faint nor fall away from Thee. Grant, rather, that tasting of Thy goodness we may ever rejoice in the innumerable and unfailing evidences of Thy love and be enabled to show forth our gratitude in faithful living.

As we walk through those days when the Church of our Lord recalls the hatred with which men hated him, may our own love for him be deepened. As we read anew the story of his cruel death, may we be moved to touch, in his name and for his sake, all life with compassion and with renewing kindness. As we remember that those who were closest to him fell away from him at the last, may we set our hearts to remain faithful both to him and to the company of his Church, gathered of those who have promised to be loving to one another for his sake and to give themselves in service to those for whom Christ died.

Grant to all who are of this fellowship, and to all who are dear to them, a gracious answer to their prayers, spoken and unuttered, which may be right in Thy sight. So order our waiting and our worship before Thee in this hour that in all the days to come we shall walk and talk, think and purpose, speak and do as those who have spent time with Thee and have learned how blessed it is to be the children of Thy love; through Christ, our Lord. *Amen.*

BOYNTON MERRILL, *The First Congregational Church, Columbus, Ohio*

FOR PASSION SUNDAY

O THOU Eternal God, who in Thy Son Jesus Christ hast come among men to suffer and die for our redemption, we lift our hearts to Thee. To Thee be glory and majesty, dominion and power, even as in Thee are mercy, forgiveness and never-failing love.

We lift to Thee grateful hearts for the life, the ministry, the gracious words, the holy and loving acts of Jesus. In Him have men of every time and place found a way of life, and a way to life. By His life have our lives been judged, challenged, guided, and made new in a peace that passes understanding. We thank Thee, O God.

Above all, O God, we thank Thee that He loved us enough to suffer and to die for us. Our little minds cannot fathom the mystery of such love, or understand its power. Yet we know that in the death of Christ for our redemption we see Thee in Thy fulness; we lay hold in wonder and gratitude upon Thy supreme self-giving. At Thy behest Christ died for us, and that is all we need to know. We yield ourselves to Thee in adoration and glad obedience.

Yet as we think upon the greatness of Thy gift, we confess in penitence before Thee the littleness of our faith and love. Thou hast called us to service in love of Thee and our fellow men, and we have followed too much the impulses of self-will.

Thou hast called us to trust in Thee, and in self-trust and self-despair our lives have been cluttered with anxieties. Thou hast called us to hope, and we have lived as those who have no hope. Forgive us, good Lord.

We pray Thee, O God, to create in us clean hearts and to renew a right spirit within us. When we faint, give us courage; when we are proud, make us humble, when we are self-seeking, increase our love; when we are indifferent to Thee and to the world's great need, help us to care. Strengthen us now, we pray.

What we ask for ourselves we ask for all Thy children. Let those who are hungry in body or soul be fed. Let those who are sick be made well, those who are downcast be lifted up. Give courage to the fearful, strength to the weak, and a new spirit to those who feel rancor or hate. Let Thy way be made known upon the earth, Thy saving health among all nations. We pray alike for our friends and our enemies, and bid Thee stir in us such friendliness that enmities may cease. Let our evil be overcome with good, O Lord.

And so we commit ourselves to Thee for the doing of Thy will. As our Lord has suffered for us, so let us walk His way of the cross. Not in boasted martyrdoms or self-pity, but in humble dedication to Thy will, we would suffer as Thou callest us to do. And may our suffering be a pathway to Thy service, our self-glorying be lost in Thy infinite glory. Use us, O Lord, as Thou desirest, and with Thee we will leave the fruitage of our labor.

All this we pray in the name of Him who is forever the Way, the Truth and the Life. *Amen.*

> GEORGIA HARKNESS, *The Pacific School of Religion, Berkeley, California*

FOR PALM SUNDAY

Let us pray.

PRAISE be unto thee, almighty God, for thy glory and power forever and ever. We hail thee as the maker of the heavens and all the morning stars, who shout for joy. We adore thee who hast framed the earth and adorned it with grass and beast and bird who tell thy praises when the dayspring from on high has visited us. We love thee who hast made us in thine own image to choose the lives we shall lead. Most of all we magnify thy holy name for thy greatest gift to us, Jesus Christ our Lord, who as thy very son, by his life and suffering with us redeemed us and opened up unto us the door to everlasting life. On this Sunday on which we celebrate his triumphant entrance into Jerusalem we too would hurry to the roadside to offer our heart's own hosannas. . . . .

Let us confess unto almighty God our sins.

O THOU who knowest our mortal weakness, here before thy grandeur and glory, before thine awful knowledge of all that we have done and all that we have been, we confess unto thee that by ourselves we are not worthy to stand with the least of these who wave their palms before thee. We have faltered and stumbled in thought and word and deed. We have striven with heated minds for the goods and the acclaim of this world which today is one man's and tomorrow is another's, which does not feed our soul, and which we can in no wise bring unto thee. In the meantime, we have rested too soon on the path of duty, and rewarded ourselves too early in the fight for right-eousness. But thou, O Lord, art slow to anger and abundant in loving kindness. As far as the east is from the west so far re-move thou, we pray, our transgressions from us. Restore unto us the joy of thy salvation and uphold us with thy free spirit, that as thy loving children and servants we may more faithfully serve thee and more manfully build for thy coming kingdom. . . . . .

Let us pray for all men.

ALMIGHTY father, hear our prayer for all our brothers thy children about the great globe itself. Visit with thy benediction the humble heart in every climate. Uphold the heads of state and all holding in their office the trust of the people. Be with the sick and sorrow-worn, and let them find at their beds the hem of thy garment. Turn the eyes of evil men from their dark designs by the holy light of the week before us unto paths of peace and the good will toward their fellow-men. . . . . .

Let us bring unto God our own prayers for the week.

DEAR God, defender of us all, we know not what to pray for and ask thy forgiveness upon our ignorance. Since we are sure that thou canst bestow upon us more goodness than we can ask or think, and even in what seem like burdens to us dost convey to our lives the rightful portion of the good servant, grant that we may pray only for thee, whom to know is to have every reward and all comforting love whereof we have need. Let us in the holy week before us so sense thy closer presence in its joys and sorrows that we may triumphantly enter the city of earthly tribulation and pass through it by thy grace to everlasting life. This our morning prayer we have asked in the name and for the sake of Jesus Christ our Lord. *Amen.*

ROBERT L. EDDY, *United Congregational Church, Little Compton, Rhode Island*

O God, Lord of all worlds, seen and unseen, transient and eternal, Soul of the universe, Creator of our bodies, Father of our spirits, to Thee we turn for strength and peace. We are children of a day; our sun has its rising and its setting; yet deep within us is the instinct of immortality, and the reach of our souls is beyond the grasp of our hands.

O Thou Who hast so mysteriously made us, that, living in the midst of time, we still think thoughts that lay hold upon eternity, we trust in Thee. Thy promises are written in our very being. What eye hath not seen, nor ear heard, and what hath not entered into the heart of man, Thou hast laid up for them that love Thee.

Thanks be to Thee for Christ our Lord, for the beauty and strength of his life, the truth of his teaching, the nobility of his sacrificial death, and for his victory! Thanks be to Thee for his life, continued in the house not made with hands, and in those who welcome his spirit and relive it now. On Calvary death slew life, and yet life was conqueror; hatred slew love and love could not be holden of hate; evil slew goodness and goodness proved the stronger. Touch our hearts with the joy of his victory.

Thanks be to Thee for those souls whom we have loved long since and lost awhile. Their lives were dear to us; their names are precious in our memories. Fathers and mothers, husbands and wives, children and friends, we remember them today. Spirit of the living God, walk among this people and see the priceless loves and loyalties cherished in our hearts, the invisible presences who worship with us. Let us not be a company of those alone clad in the body, but bring the company of unseen witnesses about us. Ah, Lord, no harm must come to them. The souls of the righteous are in Thy hands. Keep them whom we have committed unto Thee against that day.

We bring to Thee the world that needs Thee. Would that we could sing a song about love's victory there, but still we are, as our fathers were before us on the earth, the church militant, not yet the church triumphant. Lord, make us to be the church militant in nobility of spirit and sacrifice. Touch us with the wants of the needy, with the sufferings of the aggrieved, with the hurt of those who are wronged. Touch us with loyalty to great causes that death cannot stop, and wrong cannot conquer. Make us the church militant for justice against oppression, for peace against war, for righteousness against iniquity, for love against hate, for generosity against ill will.

Come close to each of us, and beyond the power of any human prayer, meet Thou our secret needs. Especially help those upon whose lips the song of triumph languishes today, who see no sunshine breaking through their clouds. Make some spirit radiant that had not expected it; surprise with hope some who have not dared to harbor it; bring life to some whose spirits are already dead, and let there be a resurrection here of love, and joy, and strength. We ask it in the spirit of the Christ. *Amen.*

HARRY EMERSON FOSDICK, *Pastor Emeritus,*
The Riverside Church, New York

FOR THE SUNDAY
AFTER EASTER—1

OUR Father, the glory of the Risen Lord has lifted up our hearts. In new assurance we reaffirm our faith in the Life Everlasting. We whose days are numbered bow before Thee who art Eternal. Because He lives we too shall live. In the presence of the empty tomb death loses its sting and the grave its victory.

In these precious days that have followed Easter Morn, we, like the early disciples, have seen the Lord. Our hearts, like the Emmaus home and the closed room, have been transformed by His presence. We have heard Him say, "Lo, I am with you alway, even unto the end of the world."

O Thou who art from everlasting to everlasting, have mercy upon us. The message of the Easter Morn warmed our hearts, and we declared, "He is risen. He is risen indeed." Grant us the grace to behold in His victory not only triumph over death but the conquest of sin and sorrow and suffering. Strengthen us, we pray Thee, Thou who out of love didst send Thy Son that we might behold Thy love in a person.

Grant, O Father, strength. We are weak as the tasks of the morrow confront us. Burdens must be borne. There is sin in high places. Tyrants seek to destroy our liberties, and the threat of war is like storm clouds in the skies. We need Thee, O we need Thee!

Come, Thou risen Lord, to us when we doubt, that we may see the scars in Thy hands, the wound in Thy side. Come to us as Thou didst come to Peter; forgive us as Thou didst forgive him, and ask us again and again, "Lovest Thou Me?" Come to us in blinding light, and so change us upon Damascus roads that we become new men in Christ Jesus. Be with us in prison hours, so that we too may sing at midnight. When we stand before insolent might, give to us the speech to declare the unsearchable riches of Christ.

Grant to us, our Blessed Lord, who art so near the Easter Morn, and yet so far, that when we face tribulation or distress or persecution or famine or nakedness or peril or sword we may know, as did the disciples of yesterday, that nothing can separate us from the love of God which is in Christ Jesus our Lord.

This we ask in his Blessed Name that we may, ourselves and through others, go and teach all nations, baptizing them in the name of the Father and of the Son and of the Holy Spirit, teaching them to observe all things whatsoever he commanded us, and do so in the certainty that Jesus Christ is to become the Ruler of the kings of the earth. *Amen.*

G. BROMLEY OXNAM, *Bishop of the Methodist Church, Washington, D.C.*

FOR THE SUNDAY AFTER EASTER—11

O GOD, our Father, God of might who dost rule over all, God of love and mercy, bless us and help us as we bow before thee in worship this day.

We thank thee for thy many blessings, for the blessings that thou dost give us day by day. We thank thee for our homes and our loved ones: hold them, we pray thee, in thy care. We thank thee for this land of ours which thou hast so richly blessed; may we follow thy way of peace and justice; may we give ourselves in the service of other peoples and help to bring justice and peace throughout the world. We thank thee for thy church, for the fellowship which unites us here in this place as we join in worship today.

We thank thee, Father, for him whom thou didst send to be our Savior and Lord. We praise thee for the living Christ, the Christ of Easter Day. In him we see thee, the God of forgiving love and saving help. In him thou hast revealed to us the life that we should live. Help us that we may follow his way, trusting thee as our Father, living with thee as thy children, loving our fellow men, seeking in all our life to do thy will.

We confess to thee our sins and failures and ask thy forgiveness. We have been too much concerned about ourselves and have thought too little of others. Give us, we pray thee, the Christ spirit of love and devotion. Forgive our worries and anxieties. May we live a life of trust day by day, knowing that all our life is in thy hands; and may the peace that passeth all understanding fill our hearts. Give us a deeper sense of thy presence with us. Help us to walk with thee, to open heart and mind to thee, and to know the strength and joy that thou canst give.

We pray for thy church, here in our midst and throughout the world. Forgive our divisions. May we know more and more and more the unity of our common faith as we seek to follow our common Lord. May we be joined ever more closely in the service of men and in the bringing of thy gospel to all the world. May thy church be the bond to unite the peoples of earth and to bring peace in all the world.

We pray thy blessing upon our own fellowship in this church. Unite us in thy service and in love for one another. May all who enter these doors know thy presence in our midst. Help us to serve faithfully the people of this community in all their needs. May our thought and prayers and gifts reach out to the peoples of other lands, to those that do not know the gospel, to those that are in hunger and want, to those that suffer from war and oppression. In thy love and mercy draw near to all who wait upon thee here this morning. Thou knowest all our needs and thy love goes to each single soul. Bless any that may be in sorrow and comfort them. Give thy guidance and help to those that are tempted. May thy blessing rest upon us in our daily work. May we see that work as part of our service of thee and of our fellow men.

Bless us in the worship of this hour and bless thy people

wherever they are gathered together for worship this day. Through Jesus Christ our Lord. *Amen.*

HARRIS FRANKLIN RALL, *Professor Emeritus, Garrett Biblical Institute, Evanston, Illinois*

FOR THE SECOND SUNDAY
AFTER EASTER

LORD JESUS, thou art our good shepherd. When we were lost in the wilderness of sin, thou didst come seeking us to return us to the fold of God. To bring us safely home again, thou didst endure shame and suffering; for us thou didst bear the lonely agony of the cross; for us thou didst yield to the cold hand of death. But for us thou didst cast death aside and rise to the glory of eternal life. We praise thee, our good shepherd, for thou hast laid down thy life for us, thy sheep.

We pray that we may know thee. Make our knowledge of thee personal and trustful. When thy voice calls us may we be quick to hear and ready to respond.

Lead us with open minds and expectant hearts into the green pastures and beside the still, life-giving waters, for we remember thy promise that if we drink of the waters of life we shall never thirst again.

Lead us in right paths, for thy name's sake. Lead us along the high paths of sacrifice and service. Lead us along the rough paths of self-denial and humility. Lead us away from the tempting paths of sin where lurk enemies that would destroy our very souls.

Lead us at last through the valley of the shadow into the

brightness of eternity. Lead us by the Cross to heaven that we may dwell in the house of the Lord for ever.

And for those other sheep which are not of this fold we pray. Bring them, too, O shepherd king, that in thee there may be one flock and one shepherd. Many are lost, yet do not recognize their plight. Find them, faithful shepherd. Find them through the ministry of the church. Find them through the work of missions. Find them through the daily witness of faithful Christians.

Many have strayed from thy flock, hardly sensing their separation from thee. Call them back by thy persuasive voice. Call them by the sting of conscience. Call them by the emptiness that only thou canst fill. Call them by the never-wearying Holy Spirit.

Deliver us all from the presumption that the narrow limits of our fold are the boundaries of thy love and concern. Give us a sense of brotherhood with thy many people, for we are all of thy flock. How casually we say that there is one Lord, one faith and one baptism—and how faintly we believe it. Grant that there shall be no hypocrisy in our hearts when we confess that we believe in "one holy, Christian church." Make us one in fact, even as we are already one in faith.

In thy blessed name we pray, our shepherd and our God. *Amen.*

PHILIP L. WAHLBERG, JR., *St. Mark's United Lutheran Church, Corpus Christi, Texas*

FOR THE FIRST SUNDAY IN MAY

When Observed as Rural Life Sunday

O LORD, our God, we greet Thee the Maker and Sustainer of all things, the Father of our Lord Jesus Christ and our Father; who, having made all things ready, dost send abroad Thy Son as servant to bid us to accept Thine invitation to come to Thee. Enable us, we beseech Thee, to lay aside our preoccupations and our concerns with the immediate and as those that want no excuse, make us free to catch the glory 'round Thy feet, free to hear the sound of Thy voice, free to claim Thy gifts which are in Christ Jesus our Lord.

Our Father, forgive us the blindness of eyes that will not see, the deafness of ears that will not hear, the cluttered hearts that have no room for Thee. Recover for us, we beseech thee, simplicity, ruggedness, and fervor, to the end that we may take that place by Thy side which Thou hast in mercy given us in Christ our Lord.

We remember Thee as the Husbandman of all life, Lord of the fruitful branch and Pruner of all that gives promise of no fruit. We remember Thee as the One who beyond all planting and watering giveth the increase. Bless, we pray Thee, all who prepare the good earth for the planting, who sow beside all waters, who commit to Thee the labors of their minds and hands. Grant the warmth of Thy sun, the nurture of wind and rain to the end that all the seed promise of good growth may be fulfilled in Thee.

We remember Thee in all Thy waiting patience. Thou dost not uproot the evil. Thou dost let it grow with the good until the time of harvest. Thou alone dost separate the wheat from the chaff; gathering in the wheat, giving to the winds the chaff. Even so, Lord, grant us willingness to wait in hope and to serve in steadfast confidence. Thine be the kingdom and the glory and the power in the church both now and evermore, through Jesus Christ our Lord. *Amen.*

FREDERICK W. ALDEN, *Minister to the Congregational Conference of New Hampshire*

FOR THE SECOND SUNDAY IN MAY

Commonly Known as Mother's Day

ALMIGHTY and Eternal Father, Thou who art our Guide along the pathway of our days: breathe upon our hearts in the quiet hours of this holy day, even here and now, that we may become truly alive to all that is beautiful and true and good. We love the holy places of this life, O Lord, and ask Thee to help us recognise this Sanctuary, these loved ones and friends, the appointments of this service, as the symbols of Thy presence, where our souls would bow in reverence and receive again the gift of Thy saving love.

Along the way by which Thou hast brought us as a people there have been so many expressions of Thy grace and care. We remember especially now our homes, where love and honor and peace dwell, thanking Thee for the ties that bind us together as families. We bless Thee for our mothers, who nourished us and cared for us when we could not care for ourselves, loving us beyond our poor powers to understand, and holding us to the highest and holiest treasures. For all the ennobling memories that gather about this day, we pray Thee to make us responsive: may they awaken within us that true chivalry of spirit that shall make us more worthy of the gift of our mothers, and send us forth as gallant sons and daughters to cherish and defend the ideals by which they lived. Shield our homes, we beseech Thee, O God, from the corroding sins that blight little children, and that break the bonds that hold us together as families. And we earnestly pray that Thou wilt deliver us as a nation from the dread threat of war; that we may seek and find both the understanding and the will that make for peace.

We bring before Thee our schools, where the tested truths of the ages are held in trust and committed to the minds and hearts of our children. We thank Thee for our commerce and industry, our fields and forests, our rivers and mountains and mines; all of which we acknowledge as gifts to be secured and shared. May it be, O God of our mothers, that through all the turmoil of our present days we shall not lose faith in our Christian purpose, or doubt the goodness of Thy hand to all people of good will. And so we would hold before Thee the larger families—the family of faith, our own and all others; the family of our nation, our own blessed land, remembering that Thou hast made us all of one blood to dwell on all the face of this earth. Bless those who have places of leadership and control, in whose hands are the grave decisions of our time, that they may have the wisdom and strength of Thy Holy Spirit.

We bring to Thee now, as in the arms of faith and love, those who are bearing the weight of years; those who are heavy-laden with illness or troubled in spirit; those who know disappointment and sorrow; all who need the tender care and assurance Thy saving Grace alone can give. Draw near to us all, we pray Thee, O Lord, as we draw nigh to Thee, that with renewed faith and devotion we may return to our places of life and labor, knowing Thee and each other in dearer company of fellowship and service. In the name of Christ, the Brother and Saviour of us all we have asked this our morning prayer. *Amen.*

Wofford C. Timmons, *Sometime Director, Congregational Commission on Evangelism; Late Pastor, Church of the Wide Fellowship, Southern Pines, North Carolina*

When Observed as Mother's Day or Christian Family Day

O GOD, who in this turbulent and changing world dost provide foundations which cannot be shaken, grant us grace to build our homes and sustain our hearts upon them.

The confusion of these tangled times bewilders us, strident voices for pride and prejudice besiege us, fears born of selfishness overshadow us. The ground of things long trusted shakes beneath our feet, landmarks long depended upon vanish, the skyline of hopes long treasured is threatened by darkness.

So it is that we have doubted Thee, wondered if there is anything to be depended upon, anything beyond the hungers of our flesh and the momentary anesthesia of their satisfaction, anything beneath and above man's selfish striving and blind groping.

But such doubt is of weakness and we are ashamed of it. We repent and ask forgiveness. For as we honor all good mothers we know love abides, as we think of all good homes we see again the skyline of redeeming hope, and as we behold Thee revealed in them we know the foundations for faith abide.

So, today, in gratitude for all that Christian homes and family life have meant and can mean, we dedicate our hearts and homes to Thee and the greatness Thou art seeking to achieve through them.

We dedicate them to the intelligence of love and the strength of faith, to the gladness of beauty and the nobility of reverence.

We dedicate them to thoughts that make us pure, to hopes that make us brave, to trust that makes us serene.

We dedicate them to hospitality which strengthens friendship and sustains the lonely, to humility which builds bridges of understanding and releases the saving grandeur of forgiveness.

So may Thy Kingdom come and Thy will be done on the earth, in our hearts and homes, even as it is in Heaven; through Jesus Christ our Lord. *Amen.*

EVERETT W. PALMER, *First Methodist Church, Glendale, California*

FOR THE THIRD SUNDAY IN MAY

or FOR ASCENSION SUNDAY

HEAVENLY Father, we give thee thanks for sending thy Son into the world for our redemption; and that by his death and resurrection and ascension into heaven He has opened unto us the gates of everlasting life and given us firm hope of the coming of thy kingdom in the world. Let our minds and hearts be fixed upon Him there with thee on thy throne as we worship together now, and as we go out to the living of our daily life. In His ascended life help us to see the promise of our own when our work here is done, and in the light of it to serve thee faithfully as He did in the days of His flesh.

For our sins and follies of the past we pray for thy forgiveness which thou hast promised to those who truly repent.

Hear our prayer for all who are sick or burdened with care, with grief over loved ones lost, with fears for the future; let the lonely be comforted by a sense of thy presence and companionship, and the tempted be strengthened by the assurance of thy aid.

We pray for thy Church throughout the world. Grant it to bear constant and fearless witness to thy eternal purpose to bring together all the nations and races into one family through

Christ, and itself to set the example by healing its divisions and achieving unity in faith and fellowship.

We pray for our country. May thy Holy Spirit enlighten and guide our leaders and all who have responsibility for the making of our laws and foreign policy. Save us from arrogance and give us the grace to think, not only of ourselves, but also of the welfare of all peoples on earth. So may thy will be done and thy kingdom come. We ask it in the name of our ascended Lord and Saviour Jesus Christ.

FRANCIS J. MOORE, Sometime Editor of *The Forward Movement*

A PRAYER FOR THE THIRD SUNDAY

IN MAY—11

or FOR TRINITY SUNDAY—1

O GOD, Father of us all, who hast created us in thine own image, we praise thee for our creation. Out of nothingness hast thou formed us, and were thy hand to be withdrawn from our lives we should fall back into the nothingness from which we came. With thy servant of old we confess, "Behold I am fearfully and wonderfully made." We praise thee for upholding us throughout life, giving us abundantly all those things needed to sustain the body, to enlighten the understanding, and to purify the soul. Deliver us from the sin of accepting life and its gifts as if they were something that we deserved. Help us to see in our very being a Father's desire to share his Being, and in our daily blessings a Father's concern for His children.

Praise be to thee, God our Father, maker of heaven and earth.

* * * * * * *

Blessed Saviour, redeemer of the world, we adore thee who by thy sacrifice on the cross hast delivered us from sin and death. All we like sheep had gone astray, each one turning to his own way. But in the wonder of thy love, thou hast shouldered our iniquity and borne it away in thine own agony and bitter death. We adore thee who by thine almighty power hast thrown down the gates of Hell and in the glory of the garden hast revealed the portals of eternal life. Thou knowest, O Christ, our stubborn pride and our selfishness, for thou didst live with us in human form. Convince us, therefore, by the mighty argument of the Cross that we need to be saved. Convict us by thy perfection that we need to be humbled. And constrain us by thy holy example to deny ourselves and take up our cross daily to follow thee.

Glory be to thee, Jesus our Lord, son of God and son of man.

* * * * * * *

Thou Holy Spirit, sanctifier of men, who in times past hast spoken to us by the prophets and apostles, we glorify thy name. As thou didst speak to inspire the writings of the Scriptures, speak to our hearts that we may believe the truth. Fan the embers of faith laid on the altar of our souls until they burst into living flame and touch with saving warmth the lives of others. Feed the fires of our faith with heavenly fuel that they die not. Inspire the ministry of the Church in every land that the light of the Gospel may shine to drive out the darkness of sin and superstition, and to blot out the shadow of war. Where the church is oppressed, her pastors threatened, and Christ's people scourged, be present as the Divine Comforter to keep men true to the faith and confident that those who are persecuted for righteousness' sake are accounted blessed in the kingdom of God.

Blessed be thy name, Holy Spirit, Lord and giver of life.
Worthy art thou, our God—Father, Son, and Holy Spirit—

to receive glory and honor and power, now and forever. *Amen.*

PHILIP L. WAHLBERG, JR., *St. Mark's United Lutheran Church, Corpus Christi, Texas*

FOR A SUNDAY IN MAY

or FOR TRINITY SUNDAY—II

ALMIGHTY God, Eternal, Invisible, whose kingdom is everlasting and whose power is infinite; We praise thee for the ineffable majesty and mystery which lie at the heart of thy Being. Truly, unsearchable is thy greatness, and thy ways are past finding out. Yet in thy wisdom and mercy thou hast given us, in thy holy Word, a light in our darkness and a sure guide toward the deeper insights of our hearts. Deep calleth unto deep: in the daytime and in the night thou art with us as a song, and our prayer answers thee, O God of our life.

Thou art Creator: Maker of the broad seas and plains, mountains and rivers, and the whole round earth; Creator of the galaxies, and of time and space; Maker of things both visible and invisible; of unseen forces and unplumbed depths which the mind of man can not yet measure; Maker of beauty, of color and form, of thoughts and visions; Creator of courage and patience and loyalty and goodwill. Made in thy image, O Father, we hear thy call to become fellow-creators with thee, sharers in thy work of finishing the universe and displacing chaos with order. In this spirit we would harness the rivers, sow the seed and reap the harvest, further the arts and sciences, make the desert blossom, build areas of beauty in the forests for the healing of the soul; for the fulfilment of thy kingdom after thine own heart. Thus may we, too, become creators with thee and for thee, whom to serve is perfect freedom.

Thou art Redeemer: Restorer of the forsaken, rescuer of the lost. For while we were yet sinners thou didst come in Christ to reconcile the world unto thyself. Thy love outran our fleeting cowardice and brought us home. Thy faith in us broke down our faithlessness. And when we learned, by the passion of our Lord, that thou accepted us, in all our stain and unworthiness, we began to accept ourselves because our trust was in thee. Where else, O Lord, could we turn? Thou art our shield and our defender. Thou understandest our thoughts afar off. Made in thy image, we hear thy call to be fellow-redeemers, to go out in love to our brothers before they repent, restoring broken friendships, forgiving from our hearts even as thou dost forgive us from the heart of the Eternal. Thus may we share in thy divine work of redemption.

Thou art the Builder of Fellowship: O Spirit of unity, binding together the blessed company of all faithful people, the Church Universal. For we are thy family, formed of thy will, the instrument of thy loving purpose for all mankind. Our pitiful brokenness offends thy plan for us, thy children. Made in thy image, we hear thy call to build with thee thy community of brothers, whose varied gifts and dreams, fitly framed together, shall grow unto an holy temple for thy habitation.

Accept, we beseech thee, our praises for the revelation which thou hast made of thyself, Father, Son, and Holy Spirit, and mercifully grant that, ever holding fast this faith, we may magnify thy glorious Name; who livest and reignest one God for ever and ever. *Amen.*

JOHN W. SUTER, *Custodian of the* BOOK OF COMMON PRAYER

MOST merciful God, our Maker, we humbly bow before Thine infinite power and majesty. Each day anew the wonders and glories of creation remind us of Thy boundless, limitless Self.

We see Thee in the universe and in the sparrow.

In the beauty of the sunset and in the freshness of the rain, Thou art there.

Thy life is in the growing grain and in a growing child.

We bless Thee for eyes to see, minds to know, and spirits to appreciate all these, the works of Thy hands. But especially do we thank Thee that we may call Thee "Father." Help us to trust completely, we pray. Remind us constantly that Thou dost care for us and that we matter to Thee. Teach, us Thy loving children, to say "Father" with all confidence and reverence. Help us to turn to Thee each day and every hour, in happiness as well as sorrow, in success as well as failure.

* * * * * *

Lord Jesus Christ, our Saviour, Son of the Living God, we thank Thee that Thou hast entered this world of men for every man's redemption.

O Christ of the Galilean hillside, teach us today, as Thou didst of old. Teach us about this life and how to live it. Flood our hearts and minds with Thy truth. Inscribe Thy Way indelibly upon our consciences.

O Christ of Calvary's Cross, forgive us today, as Thou didst of old. Truly there are times when "we know not what we do." Remind us that at other moments we know only too well. Forgive our love of the darkness. Wash us from all sin, we pray. Cleanse our spirits so that we may stand before Thee made worthy, despite our unworthiness.

O Christ of Easter Morning, our Risen Lord, help us so to

live in faith across these earthly years that at the last we may share in the Resurrection and inherit eternal life.

O Christ of the Ascension Mount, our Judge and Intercessor, look favorably upon us for all our evil ways, and finally save us and keep us forever with Thyself.

* * * * * * *

Holy Ghost, Spirit of God, we bless Thee for the promise of Thy Presence, ever with us, never failing.

Guide and direct us that we may walk the ways of goodness and act always from hearts of love.

Heal our broken lives.

Correct our spiritual and moral vision.

Inspire us to live with our highest, hidden power and to serve the Kingdom with every fiber of our being.

Break through, we pray, into the consciousness of those who rule and lead the nations of the world. Fill them with the highest sense of responsibility to their fellow men and to Thee, Almighty God.

Continue to work mightily with Thy Church and people. Lend them courage and strength for witness in this generation. Empower Thy people in their weakness. And as they are the redeeming agents of the Redeemer, maintain their faith and hope in His mission and message. Glory be to Thee, the Father, and to Thee, the Son, and to Thee, the Holy Ghost. God in Three Persons, we lift our prayers to Thee in the Holy Name of Him Who has taught us to pray together: (. . . . . . *here follows a unison offering of the Lord's Prayer.*)

ARNOLD F. KELLER, *St. John's Lutheran Church, Allentown, Pennsylvania*

FOR PENTECOST

or WHITSUNDAY

ALMIGHTY God, we gather here before thy throne to seek thy Spirit in the holy air about us. We fling away our pride and cast off the heats and fears of our mortal minds. We long for the coming again of the one true Holy Spirit upon us. Kindle our souls, we beseech thee, by thy quickening presence. Burn and purge away the rebel in us to thy holy will. Let the fiery light of thy visiting love consume all unworthy ties upon our souls.

May the light newly illumined within us now show the truth and the way of life ahead. May its steady rays cheer our hearts and disperse all enemies of the soul. Let us find also the warmth of thy love in this light. Feed its flames by thy fatherly care that we thy ministers may abide serenely in its radiant joy.

We thank thee for the gift of the Holy Spirit in our knowledge of the saving grace of the Lord Jesus Christ. We thank thee that through him we find our way to thee, to life indeed, to life eternal. We thank thee for the gift of the Holy Spirit in our new knowledge of who we are, as thy children, where we are going, as thy workmen upon earth, and what we may be, as joint-heirs of thy peace through suffering with Christ. We thank thee for the gift of the Holy Spirit in our knowledge of all men as fellow-keepers of the burning spirit of thy life and love.

We pray that the flaming tongue of thy Spirit within our quickened hearts may burn to tell all men of thee each in his own language, that all may hear, and none may doubt. Let this great light so shine in us that men may see it, and seeing it understand, and understanding glorify thee who art in heaven. Let our ministry to other men in thy name light their lives by our words and deeds.

Let us through the Holy Spirit speak boldly the lordship in our hearts of Christ Jesus. Let us be unafraid before temptation to easy wrong, to the quick salve to our conscience. Let us preach Christ in our work for this his church, in seeking out the lonely and the lost in our town. Let us serve our fellowmen in the guidance of thy Spirit, fulfilling their needs as we may and not counting the cost.

And lastly we pray that we may continue firmly in the fellowship of the Holy Spirit. Let us labor to uphold the Christian faith in this church, and to proclaim its gospel by every means to the ends of the earth. Let us uphold the faith when we break bread by asking thy grace upon it. Let us hold in common the rights and worth of all men in thy sight to walk the world with equal rights and dignity. Let us continue the fellowship of the Holy Spirit from this thy house to our homes. And from there as we go from house to house during the week, let us be borne by the gladness and the singleness of heart of the Pentecostal light. Through Jesus Christ our Lord we have uttered this, our morning prayer. *Amen.*

ROBERT L. EDDY, *United Congregational Church, Little Compton, Rhode Island*

FOR THE FOURTH SUNDAY IN MAY

*or THE SUNDAY
BEFORE MEMORIAL DAY*

OUR Father, fresh from the world with the smell of life upon us, we make an act of prayer in the silence of this place. Our minds are troubled because the anxieties of our hearts are deep and searching. We are stifled by the odor of death which envelops the earth because in so many places brother fights against brother. The panic of fear, the torture of insecurity, the ache of hunger, all have fed and rekindled ancient hatreds and long forgotten memories of old struggles when the world was young and Thy children were but dimly aware of Thy Presence in the midst. For all this we seek forgiveness. There is no one of us without guilt, and before Thee we confess our sins: we are proud and arrogant; we are selfish and greedy; we have harboured in our hearts and minds much that makes for bitterness, hatred and revenge.

While we wait in Thy Presence, search our spirits and grant to our minds the guidance and the wisdom that will teach us the way to take, without which there can be no peace and no confidence anywhere. Teach us how to put at the disposal of Thy Purposes of Peace the fruits of our industry, the products of our minds, the vast wealth of our land and the resources of our spirit. Grant unto us the courage to follow the illumination of this hour to the end that we shall not lead death to any man's door but rather may we strengthen the hands of all in high places and in common tasks who seek to build a friendly world, of friendly men, beneath a friendly sky. This is the simple desire of our hearts which we share with Thee in quiet confidence. *Amen.*

HOWARD THURMAN, *Dean of Marsh Chapel,
Boston University*

76

ETERNAL God, who dost appear to the children of time as a loving Heavenly Father, we acknowledge with gratitude the unfailing providence that orders our lives. We bless Thee, not only for the joy that lifts our spirits with the impulse of praise, but also for the disciplines of labor, of insufficiency and even of pain with which our lives are touched. Before Thee we confess that if our days held no anxiety we would not know the balm of contentment. If there were no toil we would not know the healing of rest, if there were no pain we would know nothing of the beatitude of relief. Help us, we beseech Thee, to become unto Thyself as children who are citizens of heaven because of their trust, their simplicity, and their love.

We are grateful for the fair world in which we live. Its abundance puts into our hands bread for today and for the morrow, and the beauty of the changing seasons makes wide our hearts to receive the color, the fragrance and the melody of Thy created things. Forgive us, we pray Thee, if we have been heedless of this bounty and give us to see how dwarfed and impoverished our souls have become because of this blindness.

We think with concern of all those for whom this day has not dawned in radiance and in promise, those who, despite its brightness, are shadowed by fear, distress, guilt, defeat, or loneliness. It is not Thy will, we believe, that this should be so, for the life that is given us should be the life abundant. We ask, therefore, that beyond our understanding, Thou wilt today be confidence to the fearful, relief to the distressed, forgiveness to the guilty, victory to the overborne and companionship to the friendless.

Beyond this, however, we pray that our own hearts may be so tempered by Thy Holy Spirit, that we shall be able, in all the contacts that this day may bring, to give the cup of cold water to the needy ones whose paths we share, knowing that in so doing we are doing it unto Thee.

Bless, we pray, all those today who seek to bear witness to the Truth, wherever they be, in cathedral or chapel, by the roadside or in the home, by reading of the Word, by spoken testimony to its power, by the lifting of the voice in song. Grant that the worship of all men throughout the world today, whate'er their name or sign or tongue, may be pleasing unto Thee because it is offered in spirit and in truth.

Have under Thy special providence those appointed to exercise authority over us; those upon whom the grave burdens of the world's corporate life rest so heavily. Give them, we beseech Thee, wisdom, integrity, and boldness that what they do may make straight the highway of the Lord whereon all the nations of earth may walk in confidence, in mutual understanding, in living faith and in creative love.

Spare us the strife that is the evil fruitage of the hate and distrust of men. Help us to see as clearly the sin and the folly that mislead us as the sin and folly that we see in others; and teach us hourly the lessons of forgiveness and sympathy, lest, failing to forgive men their trespasses, our Father will not forgive us our trespasses.

Enter into every heart gathered in this fellowship of worship in such a way as may truly be felt, and help us all, in this experience that brings us together before Thee, to lay up treasures in heaven, treasures that we may be able widely to share with others in the empty and cheerless hours that the coming days may bring. And return us, we ask Thee, in soundness of body and with readiness of mind to the sanctuary where once again we can meet to offer unto Thee the spoken praises of our lips and the silent requests of our needy hearts. And we shall give Thee all the praise through Jesus Christ our Lord. *Amen.*

EDWIN McN. POTEAT, *Late Pastor,*
The Pullen Memorial Baptist Church,
Raleigh, North Carolina

FOR THE SECOND SUNDAY IN JUNE: CHRISTIAN EDUCATION DAY,

or CHILDREN'S DAY

ALMIGHTY God, whose Son Jesus Christ placed little children in the midst of his hearers and said, "Let the little children come unto me," grant that we may love all who are small and helpless and growing, that we may guide and nurture them into growth in wisdom and stature and into favor with thee and with men.

Give us grace, we pray thee, to share in the mysteries of growth, that we may relive our own childhood and adolescence and therefore come to understand and to feel as do our children and youth. Let us accept them as thy children, worthy of our love even when we forget what difficulties come to them as they grow up. May we see beyond their foibles, accept their annoyances, and enjoy their new insights.

We ask thy blessing especially upon the parents of the children of our congregation. Remind us that parents are the chief teachers of faith and character, and that in homes of blessing and peace is to be found a haven of security and love. Grant to parents the moral stature and the unerring insight that will make them a light unto their children.

Bless the leaders in our church school, that in their love for boys and girls they may always show patience and graciousness. For we know that thy truth is seen in people, and in the contagious contact of person with person comes the desire to have faith in thy Son, our Savior and Redeemer.

We know, O Lord, that thou art a lover of children and that thou hast given them in their souls the power to become true servants. Give them thy grace, that they may assert their immaturity in a striving for greater maturity, that they may not remain at the mercy of every chance wind of teaching and of the jockeying of men who are expert in the crafty presentation of lies, and that they may hold firmly to the truth in love, and grow up in every way into Christ our Head. Lead them, O Lord, to true maturity, the measure of development that we mean by the fullness of Christ.

Give us, O Lord, a new generation of Christians, that this world may become truly a province of thy kingdom. Bring up statesmen of a new order, that we may be freed from the easy speeches that comfort cruel men and may become a nation that loves justice and kindness and walks humbly with thee. May righteousness roll like a perennial stream among the nations, and may peace come as thy gift to mankind.

Be with us, O Lord, in all that we do. Be with us especially in our churches and homes and schools, in our work and in our play, so that we through our common labors may be heralds of thy kingdom. Strengthen us in temptation, comfort us in our defeats, guide us in our decisions, and heal the barriers between us and other men. May we live lives worthy of our high calling, serving thee in all that we do. Let Christ live in our hearts by faith, that by grace we may be justified in thy sight. We ask this in the name of our Lord and Savior, Jesus Christ, who with thee and the Holy Spirit art one God, world without end. *Amen.*

RANDOLPH C. MILLER, *Yale Divinity School, New Haven, Connecticut*

FOR THE THIRD SUNDAY IN JUNE

A Prayer for a Baccalaureate Service

ALMIGHTY God, who makest the outgoings of the morning to rejoice, we come unto Thy Presence with thanksgiving and unto Thy courts with praise. Dispel, O God, all clouds of doubt and darkness about our earthly course; that in Thy light we may see light, and in Thy love find strength for daily need.

We remember before Thee, O God, our elder brethren, who laid the foundations of this House of Learning in reverence and godly fear. Since that time even until now hath it been in building and yet it is not finished. Grant us to enter into their labors with joy, knowing that Thou wilt fully perfect the work of their hands and ours.

We call to mind, O God, our comrades of yesterday, who stand not with us in the ranks today, yet whose eyes do behold us in eternity's stillness. Rest eternal give unto them, O Lord, and let perpetual light shine upon them.

Baptize us, O God, in this hour with a new concern for the dignity of our country and the integrity of our world. Deliver us as a nation from all pride and arrogance, and as citizens from the venom of suspicion and fear. Suffer us never to go towards good ends by evil ways, nor towards evil ends by any way.

Let Thy Father hand be shielding the young men who keep a final vigil before Thee in this place. Make them to be stern towards all forms of wrong and oppression, yet most stern towards themselves. Keep them constant in their devotion to those disciplines of mind and heart that belong to the peace of the world. Prevent them in all their divers courses by Thy light and Thy truth, that they may persevere unto the end, and in the end, through Jesus Christ Our Lord. *Amen.*

SIDNEY LOVETT, *Chaplain Emeritus,*
Yale University, New Haven, Connecticut

81

FOR A COMMENCEMENT SERVICE

Our gracious, heavenly Father, who dost enlighten the minds that seek Thee, inspire the hearts that love Thee, and strengthen the hands of all those who serve Thee: let Thy special blessing be upon this gathering of Thy people, met together in this hour of achievement to recognise and honor these, Thy young sons and daughters. We acknowledge Thee to be the Lord of all life, the Source of all truth, the Fountain of all goodness; and so we look to Thee now for that inspiration which Thou alone canst give.

We thank Thee, O God, for this blessed land of liberty; its noble history as our heritage, and its place of material and spiritual power as our possession and our trust. We rejoice especially in our free and unfettered institutions, and pray that they may ever be preserved. Bless Thou our schools and those who share in their ministry to our common life. We thank Thee for all those who have sought and found the truth, and laid it as a treasure in our hands. May we understand Thy glorious provision, even as Thou hast said: Ye shall know the Truth; and the Truth shall make you free.

We lift our prayer in earnest petition for the members of this Class: what Thou dost strengthen is strong indeed; and what Thou dost inspire is established forever. Draw these Thy young servants into the fellowship of that company who, in every age, have gone forth in the procession of Thy faithful servants. Give to them wide and beckoning horizons, resolute wills, enduring strengths and unfaltering faith.

And so through the representation of this hour, through song and symbol and the spoken word, help us to find our faith restored, our vision enlarged, and our devotion deepened; that we may go forth with confidence, believing to see the coming of Thy kingdom in all the earth. In the Name of Christ our Lord and Master. *Amen.*

> Wofford C. Timmons, *Sometime Director, Congregational Commission on Evangelism; Late Pastor, Church of the Wide Fellowship, Southern Pines, North Carolina*

FOR COMMENCEMENT

or FOR A SCHOOL or COLLEGE

Almighty and Eternal God, by whose will our lives were brought into being, by whose word we are upheld, and in whose presence we continually stand, blessed be thy holy name for all thou hast willed and spoken concerning us. Thou didst gather us into families. Thou hast led us by thy work and ways into the fellowship of them that believe, called us by name into thy service, and art ever ready by thy Spirit to fit each of us to his task in thy Kingdom.

In this hour of worship remind us of the mercies with which thou hast followed us through the years that are past. Without thy light the search would have been in vain. Without thy help the labor would have been useless. For the love we have had, for the opportunities with which thou hast provided us, for the friendships that have been formed, and for the hopes that have been born of thine, we thank thee; for every prompting of conscience, and for every vision of the Truth which thou hast revealed to us in Christ.

All of this we would this day dedicate anew to thee. Forgive us, we pray thee, for our fearful, cautious trial of the righteousness which thou hast shown us; for the things we have said or done that in other lives have hindered thy purpose; for our quick desertions, for our repeated betrayals of thy goodness. Do thou trouble us again, and be gracious to us still.

Look with thy favor upon these young men and women who would give now into thy keeping against the coming years the gifts thou hast given them. Renew in them at deeper levels than knowledge that faith which is the present evidence of things not seen. For their weakness grant them thy strength. Teach them with honesty and fearlessness to think after thee thy thoughts. Work thou in their work. Let no good promise they make be broken, nor any wrong they do, or any they shall see, continue for want of the good that would repair it. (Grant to each of them that high and continuing sense of responsibility for all that is done here, for what is given and received, for what is lost and won, as shall by thy grace make and keep them faithful in the very least as in that more with which thou wouldst entrust them.) * And forasmuch as thou dost use for thy mighty purpose such lives as are in gratitude offered unto thee, channel through them each his portion of thine own intent. We commend to thy care and guidance the head of this institution, with all those who are dear to him. Uphold him with thy hands and counsel, bestow thy spirit upon him, as upon those who labor with him in the work of administration, upon those who teach and those who learn, that together, supported by thy power, we may accomplish as thou wouldst have us what thou hast given us to do.

Remember thy church and thy people throughout the earth, and come to the world's great hurt as thou art wont to come, in those that ask of thee no more than thou wilt ever freely supply, and in the asking devote to thee their eager obedience;

* To be omitted when this is used as a Commencement Prayer.

through Jesus Christ, our Lord, to whom with thee and the Holy Ghost be glory and dominion, both now and forever. *Amen.*

PAUL SCHERER,* *Union Theological Seminary, New York*

FOR THE FOURTH SUNDAY IN JUNE

O GREAT Unseen Friend, as of old the people gathered around the Master to hear his wondrous words, so we are here in faith to hear thy voice. Speak, Lord, in the quietness of this place, in the quietness of our hearts. It is thy companionship we need, the familiar tones of the voice of Galilee we know so well. Lord, speak the homely parable to us that will make all our confusion plain, work the miracle in us that will heal us of all our diseases. And, as of old the Master passed among the folk, and they in faith stretched out their hands and touched his seamless dress, and were healed, so we now with hands of faith, we touch, we too are healed.

Help us, O Lord, to find the way by which we open the door of our hearts to the passing stranger who is known to us in the breaking of bread as Lord of Life. Come, Lord Jesus, be our guest, that our hearts may burn again within us as thou dost open unto us the word.

We thank thee, Lord, for all the graciousness and loveliness of life, for the beauty of common things, and the kindness of friends, those who love us so much better than we deserve and

* Portions of this prayer by Paul Scherer from *The Book of Prayers,* edited by Leon and Elfrieda McCauley and published by Dell, New York.

think us to be so much better than we really are. Make us worthy of their confidence in us.

For all displaced persons wandering homeless, for all discouraged souls, prisoners solitary, and those who have lost the kindly light of the intellect, we pray, for those in the fiery furnace of pain and suffering that they may find a happy issue out of all their distresses, and for the old that they may find the long years bring their own lamp of comfort with them.

We would feel thy love, that underneath are the everlasting arms, we cast our burdens upon thee. Lord, we have done all we know how. We pray our prayer, our own particular prayer. Thou knowest our plight, man of sorrows. Bend thy look of pity on our pain, as anxious and troubled, we grope in the darkness to touch thy guiding hand.

For the nation of which we are a part, and its leaders, and the guiding spirits of the United Nations, and all sorts and conditions of men, we send up our prayer of faith in them as they have faith in thee.

Help us, Lord, to do, each one of us, our small part from day to day in word and wise and kindly deed, bringing nearer the new world of good men, the church universal, the kingdom of God.

Thou rememberest us when we least remember thee, so let us enter daily life again sure of that invisible, absolutely clear presence with us, to impart to us through the days of this week wisdom, courage, and the comfort of thy love, through Jesus Christ. *Amen.*

J. EDGAR PARK, *Late President, Wheaton College, Norton, Massachusetts*

O GOD most high, whose dwelling is the light of setting suns, whose glory shines beyond the farthest star and in the humblest soul Thou hast redeemed . . . Thy love exalts our littleness, Thy gentleness doth make us great. We worship and adore Thee in Jesus Christ our Lord.

Look upon us, a company of Thy children, separated from one another by barriers of ignorance and misunderstanding, which, without Thy help, we cannot overpass. Thou, O Lord, knowest us altogether—our secret thoughts, our unconfessed desires, each hidden shame, each unrealized aspiration. Interpret us to one another. Grant us Thy love—the love that hopes all things and believes all things, the love that can overcome all obstacles and break down all barriers because it understands: in the Spirit of Christ.

O God of all good, who with unsleeping concern dost watch over Thy people, we thank Thee for Thy tender care, and for every gift of grace that Thou bestowest: for the day and the darkness, for the beauty of earth and sea and sky; for work and rest; for peace and happy contentment after toil; for the companionship of friends, and the joys of home; for the strength and skill of men and women whose inventive genius maintain our business and industry. We thank Thee for responsible government and ordered freedom; for the heroism of ordinary people; for difficulties faced and handled well. . . . for failures which destroyed our pride and threw us back on Thee . . . for seed-time and harvest . . . but especially we praise Thee for Thine infinite love in the Lord Jesus Christ, whose cross calls all the world along the way to Thee, whose Resurrection is the source of our eternal hope and the assurance of Thy victory over every evil.

God of our fathers, and our God, we praise Thee for the

87

heritage of freedom and knowledge into which we have entered, and for high traditions handed down to us by those who have gone before us. Give us, we pray, in this our day the same regard for liberty of faith and conscience as that which moved our fathers, and an acknowledgment of Jesus Christ as the only King and Head of the Church, and the supreme authority in all our public and private life. Keep this our nation in all integrity and honor. Bestow upon Thy servant, our President, the riches of Thy grace, and furnish the President's advisers, and all representatives of the people in government and in courts of law, with wisdom, courage, and devotion, so that they may be eager to discern Thy will and fearless in performing it. Deliver us from sentimentality, prejudice, or hysteria, so that in our time of power this people may be an instrument of Thy blessing to all mankind. Direct our policies of State to serve the interests of Thy kingdom. Grant us such just and upright legislation as shall protect the weak, discourage avarice and vice, promote sobriety, sound learning, and good health, and use the good gifts of Thy Providence in equity. To those who administer the law, give understanding, sympathy and single regard for that which is right in Thy sight. Inspire the leaders of industry and trade with pure standards of service. Let every medium of news be used to declare whatever is true, honest, just, pure, lovely and of good report. Guide by Thy holy Spirit of Truth our universities and schools. Uplift and purify the sport and entertainments of Thy people that all may minister to health of body and mind. Create amongst us homes that shall be citadels of love, and build up in our midst a just and righteous order of society to the glory of Thy name . . .

O God, the Lord of all good life, whose desire is for the perfect life of Thy children, accept our love for Thy children in hospital and home and use it in Thy healing and consoling work. Into Thy presence we bring those in need by reason of illness, weakness . . . sore defeat . . . those who feel un-

wanted and alone . . . those who have lately laid away their
dead and for whom life is bleak and cheerless . . . As we pray
for them in the silence, do for them exceeding above all that we
can ask or think. (*Here follows a time of silent prayer.*)

Now lift us into the light and peace of Thy presence, that
in Thy love we may be joined in one communion of the
seekers and finders of Thyself, even the fellowship of all Thy
saints in earth and heaven . . . through the grace of Thy Son
our Saviour, Jesus Christ. *Amen.*

DAVID A. MACLENNAN, *The Brick Presbyterian Church,
Rochester, New York;
Sometime Professor of Preaching and Pastoral Care,
Yale University Divinity School, New Haven, Connecticut*

FOR THE SECOND SUNDAY IN JULY

O ETERNAL God, the Creator and Preserver of all mankind,
the Father of all mercies, we Thy children yield Thee high
praise and hearty thanks for Thy goodness to us and all men:
For our creation, preservation and all the blessings of this life
we praise Thee. Thou who gavest to this earth first light, then
life, then love, we give back to Thee our thanks for all
that Thou hast thus given us so richly to enjoy: for health and
home and happy days, for companioning memories like a
walled-in garden to our troubled minds, for love's enduring
patience and for friendship's years the same, for the sure knowledge that some things are true beyond gain or loss, for suffering
which has forged our souls by hammer and by heat to understand the strength of the Cross, and above all for the revelation
of Thyself given to us in the life and love of Jesus Christ. Help

us, we beseech Thee, to show forth Thy praise not only with our lips but in our lives.

And because of Thy kind Hand in which Thou holdest us, spared and free, forgiven in failure, sustained by the touch of Thy mercy and Thy hope, we are bold to pray Thee to remember not, O Lord, our offences, nor the offences of our forefathers. From pride, vainglory, and hypocrisy, from envy, hatred, malice, and all uncharitableness; from inordinate and sinful affections, from our over-weening desire ever to have our own way in all things, to the undoing of Thy Holy Spirit, Good Lord, deliver us. We have followed too much the devices and desires of our own hearts. O God,

> *Forgive the sins I have confessed to Thee;*
> *Forgive the secret sins I do not see.*
> *That which I know not, Father, teach Thou me,*
> *Help me to live.*

And finally do Thou who hast taught us that in returning and in rest we shall be saved and that in quietness and confidence shall be our strength, take us out of the loneliness of self, and fill us with the fulness of Thy truth and love. Lift us above our common littleness and daily imperfections. Blot out our past transgressions. Heal the evils of our past negligences and ignorances, make us amend our past mistakes and misunderstandings; uplift our hearts to new love, new energy, and devotion to see the love that is there and the good that is in us. So shall we serve Thee as Thou deservedst, to give and not to count the cost, to fight and not to heed the wounds, to toil and not to seek for rest, to labor and not to ask for any reward save of knowing that we do Thy will through Jesus Christ our Lord. *Amen.*

DONALD B. ALDRICH, *Dean of the Chapel, Emeritus, Princeton University*

FOR THE THIRD SUNDAY IN JULY

O THOU who visitest the earth and waterest it and greatly enrichest it with the river of God which is full of water, visit us this day with the fulness of thy spirit that we may know the powers of the good life about us and within, and so be mingled with the ever-moving grace and good that blesses all.

We thank thee for the wondrous powers of earth and sky that sustain us, the fallow soils, the sun and rain that quicken seeds and flowers, the ripening grains that grow unto the harvest. We thank thee for the wondrous powers of our human minds and hearts, that we can remember and forecast and select our ways, that we may feel the hurt of others, that we may be ashamed and afraid, that we can laugh and sing and play, that we can reason together and together fashion a life of common good.

We rejoice that we have part and lot in the vast web of life that holds us all, all suns and stars, all elements and spirits and every living thing. We rejoice that in all the world there is no wholly severed thing or separate creature.

Yet here today we acknowledge that we have sought for separate goods and special favors, that our selfish greeds have broken the great chain of being that holds all souls in life.

We remember before thee those whose lands and homes have been despoiled by the cruelties of war or the rapacities of peace. Sustain, we pray, the brave of every race who seek a better providence for their peoples and true freedoms in their nations. May our own land be purged of those harsh ways and disrespects that dim the light of our example and hinder freedom everywhere. O thou who hast made of one blood all nations of men for to dwell on all the face of the earth, lead us so to honor all that every child of man may be brought out of darkness into thy marvelous light.

In this mid-season when fields and forests are full of the

glory of flooding life, teach us how to give and how to receive. As they who till the soil wait upon the early and latter rain, so do we wait upon thee, thou Giver of Life, with thankful hearts for all the abounding goods of body and spirit we cannot ourselves effect but only receive.

As they who sow seeds and guide the plow put forth their labors in confidence and hope, we also offer ourselves for those works of good that cannot be done save by our own doing.

So shall we share the streams of divine blessing that flow forever for us according as they flow through us and from us. *Amen.*

Von Ogden Vogt, *Minister Emeritus,*
First Unitarian Church, Chicago, Illinois

FOR THE FOURTH SUNDAY IN JULY

THE INVOCATION AND ADORATION COLLECT

Almighty God, adorable and holy, who dost govern all things in heaven and on earth, fountain of life, father of mercies, we praise and bless and worship Thee. In the full tide of the blessed summer season we give Thee thanks for the life-giving sun, for the fructifying radiance of the over-arching skies, for the benediction of the clouds, for the mercies of the dews and of the rains, for the good earth which is preparing seed for the sower and bread for the eater. Help us as we bow before Thee to worship Thee in humble reverence, in sincerity and in truth.

THE COLLECT OF SUPPLICATION FOR GRACE

O God, our Father, unto whom Thy people of old did look with trust and hope out of the midst of their danger and distress, we lift up our hearts unto Thee out of our weakness and need. Watch and wait with us by day and be our defense and guardian by night, we pray.

In our weakness, give us of Thy strength;
In our ignorance, give us of Thy wisdom;
In our pain, give us of Thy patience;
In our sorrow, give us of Thy comfort;
In our despair, give us of Thy hope;
In our trouble, give us of Thy peace.
For everything we would be thankful;
For every need we would be trustful;
In every danger we would be brave;

In every word and thought and deed, we would follow Jesus' way, and that way is Thy will; and Thy will is our peace.

THE COLLECT OF PETITION FOR DAILY NEED

O Thou who knowest our need before we ask Thee, grant us strength for the day's task whatever it may be, grant us the food needful for our life; grant us the grace to be kind, loyal, and devoted to those bound up with us in the bundle of life, and just, diligent, courteous and merciful toward all with whom we have to do along the common ways of life.

THE COLLECT OF INTERCESSION

We pray for little children and youth that they may be led into paths of usefulness and blessedness on their life's journey. We pray for the aged that for them there may be light at eventide. We pray for the sick and hurt and for those who strive to make our streets and roads safe, for those who administer our common life to the end that it may become indeed a commonweal. Let Thy Kingdom come and Thy will be done among us to the glory of Thy Holy Name, through the blessing of all Thy peoples.

THE COLLECT FOR THE UNITED NATIONS

LET Thy blessing be with the delegates to the United Nations when they gather and take counsel together concerning the things that make for peace. Give to each of them and to all of them largeness of vision, calmness of temper, the spirit of true judgment, a deep and ever-present sense of the miseries that war brings and an unwavering faith in the possibilities of human progress. Enable them to see the better way and to chart it truly for the time to come.

May Thy Spirit brood over the Conferences of the peoples, bringing out of the chaos of our disordered and bewildered world a new order of righteousness, peace, and joy in the Holy Spirit, wherein all men shall dwell as children of Thee, their God, in the Home of their Father. *Amen.*

ROCKWELL HARMON POTTER, *Dean Emeritus,*
Hartford Theological Seminary, Hartford, Connecticut

FOR A FIFTH SUNDAY IN JULY

O GOD, eternal, immortal, invisible; King and Shepherd, Rock and Refuge; our heavenly Father: We turn to Thee in need and longing and with quickened expectation. We come to Thee as to One who knoweth us altogether, who pardoneth all our offenses and healeth all our diseases. We rejoice that we may share Thy life and have such ready access to Thee who rulest over all. Thou hast set before us an open door that no one can close, and hast made us citizens already of the Jerusalem that cometh down from above and heirs of eternal life. Therefore we come to Thee with praise and thanksgiving.

We are hard beset with crowding duties, with preoccupations and anxieties. As we turn to Thee, however, we find light and direction. Thou wilt speak to us and we shall hear. We shall receive strength, and the light will fall across our path as we open our hearts to Thee, who art Alpha and Omega, the Author of our days, on whose faithfulness we lean. Deepen, we pray Thee, our confidence in Thee. We believe; help Thou our unbelief. May we move from weakness to strength, and go on from strength to strength, as we lay hold ever more firmly upon Thee who hast laid hold upon us. So may we know Thee who knowest us altogether. To this let all our doings lead. In our faithful and disinterested work among men let us serve Thee. In our devotion to the common need let us praise Thee. In selfless care for our loved ones may we exalt Thee. May we use all the occasions and tasks of life to draw closer to Thee. And in our prayers and worship may we find Thee and receive Thy blessing and solace.

Forbid that we should live a heedless life as of those that sleep, unwitting of the fateful issues all about us and blind to the hand of God in all that occurs. We would not be of those whose lives are absorbed in passing things or who live under the spell of the moment's joys. Guard us against shallowness, waste and emptiness. Open our eyes to see the deeper laws of life at work about us, to know the urgency of choice, the dire cost of refusal, the greatness that can appear in our common days. Do Thou enter Thyself into our thinking and doing, into our seeing and feeling, so that nothing remains commonplace; so that zest and endurance may be ours; so that great hopes may soar. Forbid that we should seek to live by our own strength, or by passing impulses that come and go. Give to us rather, as to those who overcome, the hidden manna that will sustain us through the longest pilgrimage. Grant us the white stone with a new name written on it, the pledge of Christ, who opens every door before us, and whose sharp two-edged sword of truth cleaves the darkness and banishes all falsehood and unbelief.

We bring to Thee, O God, each one of us, our special needs and petitions. We know not how Thou dost answer prayer, but our hearts bid us tell Thee of our cares and extremities, and the Holy Spirit inspires in us hungers and impulses directed toward Thee.

We pray that Thy Spirit will move in the hearts of men in our time towards the ends of reconciliation and peace. Bless our nation and its leaders today with soberness and humility. Renew the strength and witness of Thy Church in the common life. Grant Thy blessing in far-reaching ways to this church and to all its officers and members. As we place ourselves in Thy hand may we all find joy in our common tasks and readiness for Thy leading, through Jesus Christ our Lord. *Amen.*

AMOS N. WILDER, *Harvard Divinity School,
Cambridge, Massachusetts*

FOR THE FIRST SUNDAY
IN AUGUST

ETERNAL Father, we thank Thee that just as in the heat and dust of the town we may remember the coolness and cleanness and silence and peace of the country which lieth all around us unseen, so in the turmoil of our hurrying lives, in the midst even of pain and failure, we may remember that beyond and all around is Thyself, trustworthy, beautiful and brave, in Whom is our Hope and our Stay forever . . .

As children bring little offerings of flowers to one they love, so we bring Thee our gift of praise. Accept, O Lord, our love and quicken our spirit of gratitude that all that is within us may bless Thy holy name. For the fair beauty of spring days and for the quiet, refreshing glory of nights in August, we praise Thee. For the green banners flung against the sky, for color and fragrance of flowers, for bird song in woodland and near city streets, we praise Thee. For understanding, loyal friends and loved ones in our homes, for wise teachers and patient counsellors, we praise Thee. For our place in the forces of Christ, for the bracing fellowship of Thy Church Universal, we praise Thee. For labor and leisure, for laughter and tears, for our goings out and our comings in, guided and guarded by Thy Spirit; and above all, for our redemption in Jesus Christ Thy Son, we bless and praise Thee, O God of grace and glory!

O God who lovest all and forgettest none, help us to pray in these our intercessions that the darkness of ignorance, prejudice, misunderstanding, may be scattered by the light of truth and wisdom and kindness. O Thou who dost walk into every room and ward of every hospital, we pray for those who are sick and weak and weary, and for those who minister to them, that Thy perfect will of abundant life for all Thy children may be increasingly realized through our response. For the lonely, for those who feel unwanted, for the fearful and discouraged, we pray Thy gentle Spirit may relax all care and release healing and strengthening power. For the sorrowing, grant the assurance of Thy victory over death that they may know unbroken spiritual fellowship with their loved ones in Thee . . . O Lord of Life Eternal, we thank Thee for all who have entered into another dimension of life beyond our sight and in particular for our loved ones whom Thou art keeping and directing in the life and glory of the unseen. Keep us in fellowship with them in Christ and grant us grace to persevere in our pilgrimage by Thy loving will, until we rejoin them in Thy presence forevermore. And to Thy thrice-holy Name, Father, Son and Holy Spirit, shall we give all the glory and all the praise, world without end. *Amen.*

DAVID A. MacLENNAN, *The Brick Presbyterian Church, Rochester, New York; Sometime Professor, Yale Divinity School*

FOR THE SECOND SUNDAY IN AUGUST

O THOU Who art our God and our Father, Who art nearer to us than our breathing, and yet farther away from us than imagination can picture; Thou Who art known by each of us, and yet art beyond our understanding; Thou Who art loving and forgiving toward each of us, and yet beyond the capacity of our hearts to grasp—see us as a people who would know Thee better, who would love Thee more profoundly, and who would more faithfully serve Thee. And even when we know not for what mercies we should ask, grant them to us.

As Thou knowest how we fail ourselves and Thee, disturb us, and lead us with the assurance that with Thy help we can be better than we are. Lure us on with glimpses of the glory of Thy purpose for us and all Thy world. Hold us up in all hours of discouragement. And forgive us for our sins with a measure of justice, and with the healing affection of Thy understanding of our failures in thought and word and deed. Send us out from this place empowered to live for Thee in the week that is ahead, and in the life into which all Thy family is born.

O God, as with fumbling fingers and ill-prepared hearts we seize so carelessly the awesome powers of Thy world, teach us that we can never destroy our way into peace, show us that the dynamos for the production of good are more fruitful for mankind's unity than are the engines of war. Forgive us that we should be so foolish as to use Thy powers to make men fear rather than to make men marvel and give thanks. Set our hearts on reaching Thy kingdom above fortifying all the kingdoms of men. And beget in us as a people a new birth of devotion to the creation of a united family of nations under Thee, as once our fathers were dedicated to a united family of peoples under Thee.

See us this day as men who yearn to be better than we have ever been. For our cowardice about the good, give us Christ's courage; for our defeats, give us new purposes; for our aspiration give us new strength; for our loves enable us to find a deeper devotion, both to Thee and to others.

Here in this hour of worship, lift us all to new heights of living so that Thy Church may go on from strength to strength, —and may we come to reflect more and more of Thy life among men.

In the name of Jesus Christ, *Amen.*

FREDERICK M. MEEK, *Old South Church,*
Boston, Massachusetts

FOR THE THIRD SUNDAY
IN AUGUST—1

LORD GOD of beauty and holiness, send me forth from this place better because I came. Let this moment be unto me a moment of consecration and sacrifice—consecration of self to all things noble and fine; sacrifice of vanity, ambition and self-seeking to the greater good of someone not myself.

Here before thy face, I seek for light which is hidden most of the time. Here aspirations well up within my soul which elsewhere would be drowned in the turbulent waters of daily living. In this place there sound in my ears strains of celestial music rising through the chords of earthly symphonies to sing in my soul of things divine. Here I dare to think thoughts I would not elsewhere admit. Here before thy face I dare dream dreams at which all men would laugh or turn away in scorn. Here inside these walls of stone, under this arching roof, within this structure reared by men and called by thy name, my heart sings and my spirit soars. Here let me find, if only for a moment, all that is lovely, all that is good, all that is true, all that is holy.

Let this be my Sabbath consecration; let this be my morning sacrifice, worthy, O God, to bring before thee. *Amen.*

DUNCAN HOWLETT,
The First Church of Boston (Unitarian)

FOR THE THIRD SUNDAY
IN AUGUST—II

WE WOULD honor and praise Thee, O God, who art the Quest and Inspiration of the ages of man. We remember that all that is highest, most precious, and most beautiful in life, yea, even life itself, is the moving of Thy spirit. In manifold ways dost Thou inspire the hearts and minds of men. We would honor this day those who, in response to Thy leading, have been the penetrators of mysteries, the seekers after truth in the heart of what is familiar; those who have sought to reveal the beauty and harmony of Thy presence with words which have winged our imaginations and thoughts to the outer limits of understanding. We would honor those who have, through color and line and form helped us to feel and see the hidden beauties of familiar forms and things. We would honor those whose courage and integrity have shown forth the structure of righteousness which Thou hast established to support the universe and the lives of men with each other. We would honor those who have blended the noises of life and instruments into the harmony of music which lifts our souls into a closer communion with Thee. For all these revealers of Thy truth, Thy goodness, and Thy beauty we are not only deeply grateful, but above all we would lend ourselves to their guidance that we may find a measure of that abiding peace which Thou alone canst give. And may our moment of silent meditation bring us a new awareness of Thy presence which is ever around us and within us. *Amen.*

DAN H. FENN, *Minister, The Unitarian Church, Wayland, Massachusetts*

FOR THE FOURTH SUNDAY IN AUGUST

OUR Heavenly Father, whose light and love search the depths of our hearts, prepare us, we pray Thee, to feel Thy presence and to fulfill Thy desire. Thy greatness the heavens cannot contain, yet we find Thy nearness in those who love Thee, and most of all in Thy Son Jesus Christ. We feel small at the thought of Thy power, and yet lifted up by Thy presence. Humble us with a sense of our shortcomings and hearten us with confidence in Thy bountiful goodness and everlasting mercy. O Thou who hast waited so patiently for our prayers, forgive us for what we have been. Forgive us our coldness of mind, our hardness of heart, and our emptiness of hand. Cleanse our hearts of those secret sins which hinder our fellowship with Thee and break down the barriers of misunderstanding which keep us from comradeship with our brothers. Touch our eyes, O Lord, with cleanness that we may see through the world's falsehoods and find the truth which leadeth unto life.

Preserve our homes from petty irritations and our communities from strife. Bless our homes with patient love, our schools with sound learning, and our churches with true piety. Make glad the hearts of little children, and grant that they may grow up in a land free from war. Move the hearts of rulers to spare their peoples the misery of war and help the people in their homes to lay aside all hate and jealousy. Keep us from pride of race and wealth that we may live humbly with all men both near and far. We pray for the President of the United States that his spirit and health may be sustained. Guide the destinies of nations and grant that the leaders of all lands may pursue peace until they find the way to justice and brotherhood.

Awaken our minds, we pray, to the good things before us. Restrain us when our feet wander into temptation, strengthen us when our hands lose their grip on our tasks, encourage us when our hopes fail, and comfort us when our loved ones fall. Guide our steps that we may not wander from the road of high purpose into the paths of low desire. Lead us where we may see life's largest possibilities and keep us from stopping beside the second best. Help us to be masters of ourselves and servants of Thine. Illumine our insights with love that we may believe the best in others and consecrate our wills that we may give the best to others. Grant us to ask aright that Thy wisdom may save us from all false choices. Give us wisdom to withdraw from needless dangers and courage to confront the necessities of life. Strengthen our hands that we may be able to do the duties nearest to us. Lengthen our hopes that we may trust our tomorrows and face eternity without fear.

Grant us patience in our fretfulness, fortitude in our suffering, and comfort in our sorrows. Grant that we may lose our bitterness of soul in largeness of service that through us others may be led into the way everlasting and our world may be brought nearer to Thy kingdom of brotherhood, justice, and peace. Inspire us with the noble examples of those who have gone before us, encourage us with the comradeship of those who work beside us, and consecrate us to the welfare of those who come after us. Fortify our faith, quicken our hope, enlarge our love. Help us to be Thy faithful servants here and Thy friends forever; through Jesus Christ our Lord. *Amen.*

RALPH W. SOCKMAN
Christ Church, Methodist, New York

FOR A FIFTH SUNDAY IN AUGUST

or FOR A RETREAT

or A WORKERS' CONFERENCE IN SUMMER

O THOU God Almighty and Eternal, ever brooding over man and always coveting for him his highest good, King of all worlds and Lord of all centuries, we pray not for Thy presence now, but for the knowledge of it, the awareness of it, the assurance of it. We believe in Thee but act as if we didn't. We trust in Thee but speak as if we didn't. We know Thee but fear as if we didn't. Thou art ever near us, always present, walking daily beside every man. Yet like air and earth and water, Thou art so much with us that beholding we do not see, and hearing we do not comprehend, and touching we go our way as if we walked alone. By joy or by sorrow, by pleasure or by pain, by peace or by war, by gain or by loss—make known Thyself to us in ways which we cannot mistake. Shout in our ears, flash lights in our eyes, pour water on our faces, pinch us, stab us, trip us, push us. Smite us to save us, Lord, and hurt us to heal us; and when before the bitter cold of earth we seek the comfort of the long, long sleep in snow from which there is no resurrection, deny us peace that Thou mayest give us life. Keep us from seeking the calm which none can know but those who know not Thee. Spare us from longing for the quietness of rocks or cows. Make us restless until we find our rest in doing Thy will, and so lead us through the nights and days of earthly life, that, bearing burdens, we may bear them gladly, and, free from strife, we may seek the next task Thou dost ask of us.

Out of the silences Thou dost speak to us this day, our Father. Thou art near us at this moment—here in this sacred place where oft of old Thy people have met to praise Thy name and pray for Thy blessing. We seek Thy handiwork in everything that is. We sense Thy power in the blood that flows through our bodies, the beating of our hearts, the taking of air into our lungs. Save us from contempt for the world near at hand. Keep us from standing on the very ground of our being and saying it is not there. Protect us from bumping our heads against Thy will and pretending that we didn't feel anything. Spare us the arrogance of living daily by Thy bounty but denying we ever tasted it. We ask for faith to move mountains, our Father—mountains of selfishness, of fear and pride. Teach us the charity to say of our neighbor that if he is not against Thee he is with Thee, and the courage to say of ourselves that if we are not with Thee we are against Thee. Make us hot or make us cold, but of the lukewarm gruel we have tried so often to serve the world in Thy name, we pray that Thou have no tolerance. Be angry with us when we have called ourselves Thy people but have belied that designation. Fire us with Thy will. Lift us by Thy love. Wash our minds, our Father—clean their windows, air their unsunned spaces, dust their dark and musty corners, scrub their walls and floors until they shine as once they did when Thou didst create them long ago.

Grant us grace, O Lord, to return to the world of men, there to labor under Thy light. And when night crowds in and sight is gone, let us have no fear, but let us travel onward still in confidence that Thou art Lord both of the day and of the night and hast the power and the will to lead us safely home. Through Jesus Christ our Lord. *Amen.*

Roy M. Pearson, Jr., *Dean*
of Andover Newton Theological Seminary,
Newton, Massachusetts

FOR THE FIRST SUNDAY IN SEPTEMBER—1

The Sunday before Labor Day

O God Eternal, we rejoice that we may believe Thou art the loving Father of all the children of men. We pray to Thee in the faith that all men may become ministers of Thy great purpose, even as we believe they are sharers in Thy love. On this day we lift our hearts to Thee in special remembrance of those who toil with their hands to shape and sustain our common life. For their great contributions to the common weal we are ever in debt to them. As they build our homes, as they produce in field and factory the necessities of our common life, as they make possible our civilization today, we would pay our debt to them, not alone in their daily recompense but with understanding hearts. We pray for them at this hour. May they receive in all due measure the material rewards of their toil. We pray that there may come to them the richer satisfaction of being enabled to know that they are builders and sharers in the common effort to create a more satisfying human fellowship. May the gifts of a wise Providence be constantly translated by their efforts into an ever more abundant life for all the children of men.

We ask now, O God, that all whose ministry to life is in other varied fields of human effort shall never lose understanding or sympathy with their brethren in field or factory or home. Keep ever warm and compelling that sense of human fellowship which may more and more be in accord with Thy great sympathy and understanding. Keep us together, whatever our tasks, as fellow workers with the Divine purpose and love. *Amen.*

FERDINAND Q. BLANCHARD,
*Euclid Avenue Congregational Church,
Cleveland, Ohio*

FOR THE FIRST SUNDAY
IN SEPTEMBER—II

For Vocation Sunday

O THOU whose works are verity and judgement and all the wonders of a fair and beautiful earth, we give thanks for the daily work that each of us has to do, and the part that each of us may have in the good works of the world. We give thanks for the benefits that are spread abroad by the common labors of all men.

For those who sow fields and till the soil that there may be grass for cattle and herb for the service of man, we are thankful. We pray for husbandmen and all who provide food for the body. For all who hew beams and gather stones and build the houses of our streets and town, and shelters for all our doings; for those who weave and sew and make all manner of fabrication for human health and comfort; we give thanks. May the carpenter encourage the goldsmith, and he that smootheth with the hammer him that smiteth the anvil, and everyone say to his brother, be of good courage.

We give thanks for those who garner tidings of human life everywhere and import the goods of the mind, for teachers and scholars and those who discover the ways of the earth and the stars and all living things.

We give thanks for those who sing and dance, for poets and seers and all who show us the highest joys.

For those who are wise in the policies of state and promote justice in all our affairs, for prophets who cry shame upon social wrong and all who enlarge our thoughts of right, we give thanks. We pray for the President of our United States and all who sustain our commonwealth of freedoms and of truth.

O Thou who hast called us to be workers together with thee and with each other, we have too much labored for ourselves alone, we have not enough remembered the many in the earth who have put forth their strength, yet suffer want. Guide us and teach us, we pray, to understand our times and know how best to use our talents and how rightly to divide the harvest. Help us more fully to see the duty of all to bring forth the fruits of useful living and the right of each to the just rewards of his industry.

Here in thy presence, we rejoice in the might and virtue of men in their daily toil, that day by day in all parts of the earth, men of every tribe and nation go forth to their work until the evening, for these maintain the fabric of the world and by the faithfulness of their labor is everyone blessed.

We pray in the spirit of him who said, My Father worketh hitherto and I work, whose voice speaks to us still, Greater works than these shall ye do because I go unto my Father. *Amen.*

Von Ogden Vogt, *Minister Emeritus,*
First Unitarian Church, Chicago, Illinois

FOR THE SECOND SUNDAY
IN SEPTEMBER—1

After the Summer Holidays

Infinite Spirit, who art beyond the range of sun and star and yet known to each one of us with an intimacy that words cannot express, we lift to Thee now our songs of praise for all the blessedness of life and our prayers of aspiration for the days that lie before us, humbly confessing our failures but resolutely renewing in Thy presence our determination to maintain our best endeavors to redeem the past and to live worthily as Thy children and the servants of Thy will.

As we return to this place where, through many years, Thy people have sought to worship Thee in spirit and in truth, may all the new power that has come to us in the days of the holiday season be dedicated to the noblest purposes of Thy service. May the beauty of the earth and the splendor of the skies, which have brought us rest of body and refreshment of spirit, constantly remind us of Thy promise that those who wait upon Thee shall renew their strength. May the sense of vigor that the long summer days have built up within us now remind us of Thy matchless energy upon which we may call whenever our own power falters and our human frailty brings a sense of discouragement. Help us to keep the health of mind that will direct us wisely along the sometimes darkened ways of the world. Let Thy word be as a lamp unto our feet.

Teach us, we pray Thee, to make this church a center of divine influence, where tired hearts may directly know the assurance of Thy strength, where eager and expectant souls may find without measure the touch of Thy guidance, and where in our common devotion to Thy kingdom we may all find the peace that will send us out into life with restored courage and faith. *Amen.*

FREDERICK MAY ELIOT, *Late President*
of the American Unitarian Association

FOR THE SECOND SUNDAY
IN SEPTEMBER—11

O GOD our great and gracious Father, we are glad to resume on this day our active life together as Pastor and people. We rejoice that Thou has been with us while we were sundered in the months just past. And we ask Thy blessing upon this new year in our Church, that, as we carry on at the varied tasks of Thy Kingdom entrusted to our care, we may grow daily in wisdom and power, and may be made fruitful in all our labors by Thy might working with us.

We commend to Thy care the absent members of this household of faith. Grant them Thy grace, wherever they may be; and of Thy mercy restore them to us in due season. We crave Thine aid also for all men everywhere upon whom the distresses of this mortal life lie heavily. Comfort them, O Lord, and deliver them, through Thy lovingkindness revealed to men in Christ the Universal Saviour. Bring all who are in darkness of spirit to Him who is the Light of the world.

Almighty and most merciful Lord, we beseech Thee to have pity on our weakness and show mercy towards us and all men. We confess with shame and repentance our many transgressions of Thy law and our consciences. Remember them not against us, O Lord. Move Thou upon the minds and wills of all men everywhere, that they may have heart and strength to obey thy commandments. Grant us power to discern and remove all that makes for needless strife and woe on earth.

May Thy Church Universal be indeed the living body of Jesus Christ, redeeming the world into oneness of understanding and loyalty. As we members of that body have fellowship with him, may we see also through him a unity with one another which shall transcend all racial and national barriers, creating in us and kindling in others genuine good will, a passion for righteous peace, and a dynamic longing for the general practice of human brotherhood.

Finally, O God, in gratitude for all that our Lord Jesus Christ has done for us and is to us, may we for His sake do those works of righteousness and kindness to which the hour and the need shall summon us, through the Church year now opening; that the power of faith and love may be manifested in us, and that the hearts and hopes of all men everywhere may be drawn to Thy Son, the Prince of Peace, in whose holy Name we pray. *Amen.*

RUSSELL H. STAFFORD, Sometime President of the Hartford
Seminary Foundation, Hartford, Connecticut

*or FOR THE OPENING OF A SCHOOL OR
COLLEGE YEAR*

ALMIGHTY and Most Merciful God, humbly because of our unworthiness and the wrong that we have done, but boldly because of Thy goodness and the ceaseless patience of Thy love, we would bow our heads before Thee in silent adoration. . . . Thou hast created us, preserved us, and brought us to this day, holding out to us when we were most alone the offer of Thy companionship, in weakness ministering strength, for darkness, light, remembering us Thyself forgotten, Friend to all our unfriendliness. We thank Thee that Thou hast revealed Thyself to us in the orderliness of the universe which Thy hands have fashioned, Thy majesty in its vast distance on distance, Thy nearness in the Word that comes stealing out of that silence into our hearts. The long past echoes Thy name in our ears, from prophet and saint, apostle and martyr, in the march of the years and the destiny of nations: grant us to hear Thee now speaking to us by Thy Son, and in Him to know Thee as Thou art, entering into this life of ours to bear Thyself the weight of it, forever merciful in Thy judgments, and just in all Thy compassion.

Bear with us as we confess our sins before Thee: the selfishness that changes even our good into evil, the prejudice that blinds us, the indifference that keeps us from the knowledge of Thy will, and shuts up from the homeless and the hungry the warmth of human kindness and the very bounty of Thy providence. Thou canst not heal the world's hurt if we will not be healed. We ask of Thee this day for Thy pardon and for the grace that will make us whole. Cleanse us of the wrong that distorts the mind, of the wilful desire that twists life away from

Thy purpose, of cherished hatred and thoughtless contempt, of pride of place, and of envy. Bring us in every moment of decision to set before Thee the choices we would make, submitting our knowledge to Thy wisdom, and yielding what we are to the service of what Thou wouldst have us be.

And as we pray for ourselves, we pray also for others; for those whom we call our enemies, for the sick and the destitute, for the oppressed and outcast of all peoples, for the victims of war and famine, for those who toil in mine and field, in engine-room and shop, with so little recompense from us, their names unknown, the debt we owe them scarcely recalled, never a burden on our hearts. Comfort, O God, with our comfort these comfortless of Thy children. Add to Thine own the strength Thou hast given us to gird them, and to Thy provision for their need that with which Thou hast provided us.

Have regard, we beseech Thee, to all our schools and colleges, that they may be dedicated in Thy fear to every pure art, and to useful learning, whereby life may be enriched, the bond of ignorance and superstition broken, dullness sharpened into insight, and wonder into reverence. Rid us together in this uneasy world of all that makes for enmity, of narrow loyalties that breed war, of the cramped horizons where our spirits grow poor. And rule among the affairs of men everywhere to the establishment of righteousness, and in righteousness of peace: that Thy mind may be brought by our hands into the future, not in trembling under Thy wrath, but in willing obedience; by Thy grace in Jesus Christ, to Whom with Thee and the Holy Ghost be glory and dominion both now and forever. *Amen.*

PAUL SCHERER, *Union Theological Seminary, New York*

FOR THE THIRD SUNDAY
IN SEPTEMBER

ALMIGHTY God, our Heavenly Father, we come to Thee in worship, the great event of our week. Give us a sense of anticipation and help us to be filled with expectation. We claim the promise of Jesus, that when men gather together in his name, he is there. It is in his name that we meet, and it is through him that we approach the Throne of Thy Grace.

Thou knowest that in the busyness of our lives we sometimes forget Thee. But do not Thou, O Lord, forget us. For it is in Thee that we move and live and have our being.

We could not come to Thee if Thou hadst not first sought us. We rejoice that we have been found by Thee, and that without fear we may enter into Thy presence. We are so aware of our sin and so conscious of Thy holiness, that all our pride is humbled and our hearts are filled with the wonder and mystery of Thy goodness.

We are not content with our record, and our sins are ever before us. When we consider the extent of our failure, we are prone to yield to despair. In our own strength, there is no hope for us, and we feel that health is not in us. We are not self-sufficient nor are we able to accomplish what we desire in our own best moments. Who can deliver us and who will save us?

Then we come into the Temple and Thy presence fills it, so that we can feel power flow into us. Underneath us are the everlasting arms. Our little strivings are so futile, but the sense of Thy power offered to us through Jesus Christ strengthens our purpose and steels our wills.

When we look back over our own poor lives, how can we doubt the amazing grace of Christ? Who can doubt Thy providence? We have walked in danger and Thou didst bring us safely through it. We have been close to the abyss and

Thou hast protected us. We have been so close to moral disaster, and Thy voice warned us and guided our steps.

Now, O God, bless all who grope blindly. We do not ask to know all the mystery of life, but give us light enough to live by, and show us the way one step at a time. Save us from worry about the future, and teach us how to live in faith day by day. Grant to us the confidence that trusts Thee so completely that our minds are at peace and our hearts are quiet.

Bless, we pray Thee, those who are tempted. Teach us how to flee to Thee for safety, and how to take refuge in the mighty fortress of God. Bring the power to forgive to those who are filled with bitterness and hatred. Heal the sick of mind and body so that we may testify to Thy saving health to all men.

Make this service a good one for every worshipper. Let us leave not as we came, but with a new vision, a deeper assurance, a greater hope. Speak through the sermon and the hymns, the scriptures and the prayers. Then bring to each waiting child of Thine the sense of hearing that can comprehend the still, small voice.

Hear us in the name of Jesus Christ who is our redeemer and our Lord. *Amen.*

GERALD KENNEDY, *Bishop of the Methodist Church, Los Angeles, California*

O FATHER of us all who hast given us the mercy of the night's rest and the challenge of the day's work, we praise Thee whose greatness is beyond our knowing, and whose nearness is beyond our doubting. We thank Thee for every day of life, for Thou dost bless it beyond our measuring. In the love of the family, in the spur of work to be done, in the whole changing drama of the natural world, and in the unfailing intuition of things to come, Thou dost bid us to stand free and strong. We are reminded that it is better to know Thee even in part than to know lesser realities even to the full.

Before Thee, O God, we come in concern for the Church of Christ. In this hour when out of their insecurity men speak in anger and resort to violence, grant the Church solid ground on which to stand for the preaching of the gospel. In the hour when charge and counter-charge only reflect our deep-laid fears, grant us such respect for truth that we shall never cheapen it to please men. Grant to us, too, such respect for men that we shall never use the truth as an instrument of personal power for domination. Let no cowardice prevent our speaking nor fear bind our acting. May wisdom be given to see today's issues against the perspective of time. Endow Thy Church with the gift to discern the real from the unreal, the biased from the true, the special pleading from the prophetic word. Restore the gallantry and abandon to our obedience that in a day which will be saved only by a daring faith we shall escape the lure of petty snares. Alone we are not sufficient for these things, but in Thee there is sufficiency for Thy Church.

We remember that always Thou dost stand at the door of every life. Surely Thou art seeking to come into our lives this morning, yet often we do not know that it is Thee who art asking us to open our lives. We have not expected Thy coming in such ways—in the pain which teaches us the limitations beyond which we may not go, in the hunger which will not be satisfied by earthly things, in the challenge to the unchallenged ways of thinking, in the revealed insufficiency which makes us one with all other men. Forgive us that we have not known that such instruments may be held by Thy hand. We only can thank Thee, love Thee, and trust Thee. So, in the holy solemnity of this hour, our reverence rises again at the revelation of Thyself in Jesus Christ, our Lord. *Amen.*

GENE E. BARTLETT, *First Baptist Church, Los Angeles, California*

FOR THE FIRST SUNDAY IN OCTOBER

World Communion Day

CREATOR and Companion of our souls, who hast made us for Thyself so that our hearts are restless till they find rest in Thee, may we now be quiet before Thee and responsive to Thy touch. Let there be an inner hush of spirit amid the outer rush of things. In the face of confusion all about us may there be peace within.

> *Dear Lord and Father of mankind*
> *Forgive our feverish ways,*
> *Reclothe us in our rightful mind,*
> *In purer lives Thy service find,*
> *In deeper reverence praise.*

May our renewed fellowship with Thee inspire us to more faithful living in all the common round of duty and pleasure. May our daily work and relationships all be hallowed by a sense of Thy purpose for our lives. So walk with us through field and factory, through office and store, through home and school and hospital that whatever we do may be a witness unto Thee.

We bless Thee for the fellowship which we have in the Christian Church with the whole family in heaven and on earth. We rejoice that it links us with saints, apostles, prophets, martyrs, and the goodly company in all the ages who have loved and followed Christ. We praise Thee also for a fellowship which reaches around the globe and unites us with men and women of every land and clime who have found in Christ the true meaning of life. May we in our own time and our own place be worthy members of this glorious fellowship.

Lord of the Church, who has chosen it to be the Body of Christ, grant that in all its life it may faithfully reflect His spirit. Keep it full of Christ-like compassion for human need. Make it sensitive to every cry for justice and for freedom. Save it from complacency with anything that is not in accord with the mind of Christ. Let it never be weakly conformed to the patterns of the world around it. Grant it the prophetic insight and experience which will make it bear witness to Christ's transforming power. So may the Church in our time be a foretaste of Thy Kingdom, embodying in itself the love and the holiness which Thou hast revealed in Christ as the way of life for all mankind.

To Thy whole Church throughout the world grant a deeper understanding of what Thou dost mean it to be—a redeemed community out of every race and nation and tongue, acknowledging one Savior and serving one Lord. Help it to overcome all divisiveness within itself and enable it to keep the unity of the spirit in the bond of peace. Through Jesus Christ, our Lord. *Amen.*

SAMUEL McCREA CAVERT, *Executive Secretary, Retired, The World Council of Churches, in the United States*

ALMIGHTY God, Father of our Lord Jesus Christ, who art always more ready to hear than we to pray, and art wont to give us more than we either desire or deserve, attend, we beseech Thee to the voice of our prayer and regard in Thy mercy Thy people gathered together in Thy name.

We thank Thee that Thine ears are always open, that Thy heart is always tender. If we have forgotten Thee, Thou hast not forgotten us. We have erred and strayed like lost sheep. Yet Thou dost always seek us and fetch us home again.

We bring to Thee the thirst we cannot quench from any earthly spring, the hunger which Thy love alone can satisfy. Lift us out of our shadows into Thy light, out of our fears into Thy peace, out of our perplexities into the certainty of Thy truth, out of our foolish and wayward purposes into Thy blessed will in us and for us.

Forgive us, we pray Thee, for sins remembered or forgotten; for our misusing of Thy good gifts, the opportunities neglected, the unselfish deed withheld, the kind word left unspoken. We poor sinners beseech Thee to hear us.

We offer prayers of thanksgiving for Thy goodness to us so far beyond all we have deserved of Thee. For all blessings, temporal or spiritual, which daily we have received from Thee, make us duly thankful. Above all, we adore Thy mercy that Thou hast sent into the world Thy Son, our Saviour Christ, who hath redeemed us and all mankind from sin and from death. Cause the pure light of Thy Gospel to shine in all the world, and may all who receive it live as becomes it.

Have pity, O Lord, upon us Thy children, so slow to learn of Thee the lesson of brotherhood and peace. Rebuke selfishness wherever found, strengthen virtue in the hearts of all

Thy people. From the curse of war and all that begets it, good Lord deliver us. Grant special gifts of wisdom, patience, and strength to all those to whom have been committed the government of the nations, that peace, justice, and brotherhood may be established among men.

God of all comfort, we commend to Thy mercy all those who are in trouble, sorrow, need, sickness, or any other adversity, especially those known and dear to ourselves. May they receive from Thee consolation, peace, healing, and deliverance.

Hear us in the stillness of this hour and may the benediction of Thy presence be the portion of all Thy children who here have called upon Thy name. In all our duties, grant us Thy help; in all dangers, Thy protection; in all our uncertainties Thy counsel, in all our sorrows Thy peace. Through Jesus Christ our Lord. *Amen.*

RAYMOND CALKINS, *Pastor Emeritus,*
The First Congregational Church, Cambridge, Massachusetts

FOR THE THIRD SUNDAY
IN OCTOBER

OUR God and Father, who biddest Thy children call upon Thee for Thou wilt answer them, and turn unto Thee for Thou wilt bear them up, and make their home in Thee for so wilt Thou abide within their hearts: Hearken now to the prayer of our lips and fail not, we beseech Thee, to attend those wordless prayers which we know not how to utter; that, even as we lift our voice to Thee, Thy merciful bestowal may far exceed our asking; that, in this moment when we seek Thy face, we may be strengthened and restored in Thine own image; and that, throughout our days, we, casting our care upon Thy loving carefulness, may find within our souls Thy light and peace and joy.

Most loving heavenly Father, who delightest to pardon and to have mercy: Remove far from us our shortcomings and offenses, both of deed and of spirit; deliver us from negligent forgetfulness of Thee; cleanse our consciences of old wrongdoing; and mercifully establish us, renewed and gladdened, within the sunlight of Thy face.

God of all goodness, by whose might all things were made, and of whose love all things that Thou hast made are tended: Accept our offering of praise for benefits beyond our reckoning, wherewith Thou hast encompassed and enriched us. Hast not Thou loved us into being, and walked beside us all our days, and broken to us bread of time and of eternity, and healed our wound, and Thyself borne the burden of our sins, and freed us in Thy vast forgiveness, and touched our dust-dimmed eyes with sight and blessed us with immortal hope? Enable us, who cannot praise Thee as we should, because our thought is fragile and our lips are of a moment only, to glorify Thy holy Name in dedicated lives and self-forgetful deeds.

God of the Church, who graciously hast promised that never wilt Thou leave Thy congregation comfortless: Endue Thy ministers with fortitude and wisdom, and plentifully visit all Thy people with encouragement. Especially we pray for those, wherever they may be, who, for sake of faithfulness, endure loss and grievous trial, and know not what to do. Stand Thou beside them in their tribulation. Comfort them in their distress. Be Thou to them sufficient in every insufficiency.

God of the world, who turnest the wrath of men to praise Thee, and who art found of them that seek Thee not: Rescue from the blindness of a selfish will, and from the terror of their own device, the nations of this earth, and lead them, under Thy wise providence, away from violence and warfare, into peace and righteousness; that all mankind may glory in Thy great deliverance, who alone makest us to dwell in safety.

God of the whole family of men: Draw near to every man, according to his need. Be Thou Companion to the lonely, Home to the homeless, Teacher to him who would be taught, Emancipator to the hopeless, and strong Defense to him whose strength has failed. And all whom we forget do Thou remember.

Keep us, O Lord, throughout this day, and all our days; and grant that we may joyfully embrace Thy good and perfect will; through Jesus Christ our Lord. *Amen.*

JOHN UNDERWOOD STEPHENS
Former Minister of the Mount Washington Presbyterian Church, New York City

FOR THE FOURTH SUNDAY IN OCTOBER

ETERNAL Spirit, whose dwelling is in the light of setting suns, yet makest Thy home no less truly in the humble and contrite human heart, accept, we humbly pray, this our act of worship. Instruct us in Scripture, inspire us in music. Bless us in prayer, we ask, O Lord, not with our own or any lesser benediction, but with the blessing of Thy approval.

In penitence we confess that we have not, since last we worshipped here, fulfilled all our good intentions. Measured even by what we know about ourselves, to say nothing of what Thou knowest about us, who lookest upon the inmost heart, we have been unworthy and unprofitable servants. So again we confess our shortcomings and acknowledge our sins. Strengthen and renew again, most patient Father, our intent and will to do right, that in this new week our thoughts, our words, our deeds shall wound Thee less and please Thee more.

Relying utterly upon Thy grace, we would intercede for all those among us and in the world upon whom heavy responsibilities fall. Grant to each man in his work and each woman in her home a sense of holy vocation, that each of us may know the place he stands as a place of service for Thee and for our fellowmen. When we must make decisions, help us to make them not from expediency but from conscience.

In the giant complexities of our world, where untold good or frightening disaster may arise from our smallest word or act, give, we beseech Thee, a spirit of right and godly judgment to all in authority in every land. Strike down with Thy righteous wrath, O God of justice, every selfish or unfriendly gesture—our own or another nation's—that all Thy children may live in peace as brethren, and grieve Thee no more by fratricidal conflict.

As we have asked Thy blessing upon us who worship here, so wilt Thou, we pray, be with all others of Thy name or sign who this day shall assemble to pray, and to praise Thy name. Likewise of Thy goodness visit with Thy Spirit those kept from worship for any cause—by reason of needful work, by reason of illness or adversity, or from their own sloth or indifference. Forgive those who need forgiveness, even among us, and bestow Thy rich blessing upon every seeking, longing, searching heart.

Because we know only most imperfectly what to pray for, and how to pray, correct whatever is amiss in these our prayers, and grant that day by day we may learn how to make our desires worthy of being made into prayers, our prayers into deeds, our deeds into character—all to the glory of Thy holy name, and in obedience to the teaching of Jesus Christ our Redeemer. *Amen.*

> ELMER S. FREEMAN, *Sometime Secretary,*
> *The Congregational Commission on Evangelism;*
> *Pastor, The First Congregational Church, Montevideo, Minnesota*

FOR A FIFTH SUNDAY IN OCTOBER

ALMIGHTY God, creator of all things visible and invisible, sustainer of the universe and of all our hopes, we give Thee humble thanks that Thou who hast set the planets on their courses, dost also mark the sparrow's fall. Though Thou art from eternity to eternity, Thou art present in all Thy fullness here and now. We praise Thee with gratitude from the deep places of our heart that by Thy grace, in measure related to our deserving as ocean to grain of sand, Thou hast opened to us all the opportunities of the life before us. We lay before Thee our needs and our desires. Quicken our minds, we pray Thee, that confronted with the confused alliance of good and evil, right and wrong, true and false in our environment, we may have insight to select whatsoever things are honest, whatsoever things are just, whatsoever things are pure, whatsoever things are lovely, whatsoever things are of good report, and if there be any virtue, and if there be any praise, to think on these things. Touch our hearts, we beg, so that our sympathies may not be coffined in the narrowness of our own interests and ambitions, but extended to strengthen the hopes and dispel the fears of all who are in need throughout the world—the hungry of body and of spirit, the shelterless and the wandering, and all who dwell in the shadows of ignorance, uncertainty, and deception. Grant us, in the community in which we live, to be numbered among those who overcome its evil, who are the channels through which goodness, truth, and beauty are mediated from Thy heaven to the common places of our daily life. In all things give us the unquenchable hope which belongs to those who know Thee. We remember that Thy loving will must at last prevail, Thy kingdom come. Fasten our eyes upon this certainty which no earthly failure or disaster can obliterate. Though we cannot know how Thou wilt use our work or with what measure of success it will be attended, of this we can be sure, that Thou art God, and that because Thou overrulest all our tangled history, already made or to be made, we can be secure against despair and with confidence expect that all we build upon the foundations Thou hast laid will stand. Help us therefore not to set limits to our dreams but to unite each his own dream with that of him who saw a new world descending out of heaven from Thee. Temper us to live and work as those who know that Thou reignest, undaunted by the pretensions of evil or the fears of difficulty. Give us to live in lives apparently hopeless as those whose hope is indestructible. *Amen.*

DOUGLAS HORTON, *Dean of Harvard Divinity School, Cambridge, Massachusetts*

FOR REFORMATION DAY

or THE SUNDAY BEFORE

ALMIGHTY God, by whose progressing revelation our fathers' fathers came to know Thee; hear our prayer as we stand today in Thy presence and their memory.

For the guidance of Thy spirit in the lives of men of old so that wisdom and courage were found for new adventures; we praise Thee.

For the unbroken continuity of filial training in church and home, holding Thy people close to Thee in changing circumstances; we praise Thee.

Accept, O Lord, the gratitude of our hearts for the work and prayer of brave men who in earlier times have counted all else vain if they knew not Thee:

For John Hus, John Wyclif, and Gerhardt Groote who shed Thy light abroad amongst their peoples and knew the price thereof;

For Martin Luther and his comrades who for a purer faith and obedience counted life itself a cost none too great, and found Thee in freedom and in faith;

For John Calvin, John Knox, John Milton and Oliver Cromwell, who wrought a mighty work to free Thy word again;

For men of Zurich and the Rhineland, for George Fox and the companions of his quietness, who gave Thee back Thy sweet silences;

For unnamed and unnumbered men and women who stood steadfast under oppression, gathered devoutly in meeting houses, transformed the civil government, nurtured education, and lighted the light of human betterment in the world.

By faith they found Thee; in thought they discovered Thy way; in courage they obeyed Thee; in fellowship they worshipped Thee; in peace they waited for Thy final summons.

Thou wast to them the pillar of cloud by day and fire by night. So to us their descendants be Thou the unfailing guardian of our way.

And now, O Lord, grant us, the inheritors of their work, the grace to be as brave and free in following the new light which Thou hast for us. Teach us to honor them, but to follow Thee. In Thy truth and not in theirs may we see our way and come at last to find that they and we are one in Thee. *Amen.*

Edwin P. Booth, *Boston University School of Theology*

FOR THE FIRST SUNDAY IN NOVEMBER

Eternal Spirit, full of mystery beyond our understanding, yet never far from any one of us, open our lives now to Thy presence and persuasion. Approach us through the calm of this quiet hour when our spirits grow still and we can hear Thee speak. We live in troubled times, and we need Thy saving help. Grant us some fresh vision as we worship Thee, some divine visitation of new strength, some sight of Christ that will call out our responsive loyalty and draw us to nobler aims and better living.

Far beyond the borders of this congregation enlarge the fellowship of souls in whose company we worship Thee. Join to our number our loved ones on earth far away from us today but near in spirit. Make real to us the Church Universal, the Elect Spirits, both militant here and triumphant in the World Unseen, that we may be enriched in their companionship. So lift up our hearts and strengthen us to face tomorrow's world!

Especially, we pray for courage. O living Spirit, walk through this congregation now and lay Thy hands on men and women outwardly placid and serene, but inwardly whipped and beaten. For life has laid heavy burdens on some of us; death has come into our households; some whom we love best are in perilous places; all of us have hidden anxieties and fears. We need the spirit of our sires who revealed the splendor of their souls when days were difficult. Speak to us, saying, Be not afraid!

We pray for our families. Thanks to Thee for gracious and saving memories of mothers and fathers who made childhood lovely to us! As the years pass we would keep the inspiration of their presence; though they dwell in the World Unseen, may they be still our comfort, guidance, strength! Grant Thy special benediction on all here who love each other and plan homes together; on those to whom have come the privilege and responsibility of children; on those who have grown old and look now to the evening of life together; on those who have laid their best loved in the grave and think of past days and of high eternal hopes. O God, for all that concerns our families we pray to Thee from whom every family in heaven and on earth is named.

For the Church we pray. May the crisis of the world clear her vision that she may see small things as small and great things as great. From the trivialities that obsess her, the sectarianism that divides her, the loss of great convictions that enfeebles her, and the selfishness that narrows her message and her service, may the Spirit of Christ deliver her! Make this church, we beseech Thee, a loyal servant of Thy cause! To the ministers and to the laymen and laywomen of this congregation, grant vision and dedication, wisdom, generosity and devotion, that we here, a company of Christ's people, may exhibit His Spirit, do His work, and further His Kingdom!

Especially we pray that in all our labor for a better nation and a better world, even in these difficult days, we may have the gift of radiance, an inner light that shines even in the darkness. Grant us inward victory, like His who amid His griefs said to His disciples, Be of good cheer! Grant us zest in living that no grimness of the times can take away and resilience of heart that no fears can destroy. So help us to bear living witness to the triumphant grace of Christ.

In His name we make our prayer! *Amen.*

HARRY EMERSON FOSDICK, *Pastor Emeritus,*
The Riverside Church, New York

FOR THE SECOND SUNDAY
IN NOVEMBER

O LORD, Who hast been the dwelling-place of Thy people in all generations, Who art still our strong habitation whereunto we may continually resort, and Who dost bid all who are weary and heavy-laden, we draw near to Thee now, and remember with thankfulness the way by which Thou hast led us. May our worship be acceptable in Thy sight, and may Thy mission be reflected in our service.

O eternal God, our Father, Who didst send Thy Son to seek and to save the lost—deliver us from the bondage of self.

From the blind skill that has no understanding, the knowledge that has no wisdom, the glib speech that has no vision, from the heartless brain and the brainless heart . . .

From the black chaos that blasphemes creation,

From the disordered will that spews out judgment,

From the dark greed that binds us in subjection to our desires,
Deliver us, good Lord.

From the proud virtues that are our undoing,

From the harsh righteousness whose name is murder,

From the liberality whose name is treason,

From the weak and the strong, from our right and our wrong, our worst and best,

Deliver us, good Lord.

From all the gods made in the image of man,

From all the worship of man in man's own image,

From the corrupt alike and from barren imagination,

Deliver us, good Lord.

From all unwillingness to learn Thy will,

From clinging to our own plans and desires,

From cowardice in following Thy leading,

From ever suffering our own ambitions to cloud the visions of Thy will for us,

From fearing new truth and new ways of thought and life,

And from seeking to set forward human progress, whether in the church or in the world, by doing our own will instead of loyally asking to do Thine,

Deliver us, good Lord, and as with the saints of old, comprehend all our needs with Thy amazing love and strengthening grace.

O blessed and eternal Father, Who art the Author of our life and the End of our pilgrimage:

We pray Thee for the quiet mind which, in the midst of hurry and turmoil, can at any time turn directly to Thee and be immediately at peace;

We pray Thee for the enlightened imagination which gazes through form and delusion to reality, perceiving unerringly those eternal truths of the spirit which lie behind the pasteboard scenery of this world;

We pray Thee for the mastered will which attunes us spontaneously and unconsciously to Thy will;

We pray Thee for the life that is hid in Thee, the life that demands nothing for itself, but is wholly content in showing Thee forth to men;

We pray Thee for the stalwart faith which gives unto us, while still we live here on earth, the facts and substance of eternal life;

We pray Thee for all spiritual blessings, for our deepest heart's desire, and that Thy judgment may rest on all the things we do. And then, as with the saints of old, gather up all our prayers with Thine endless concern and gracious benediction.

In the name of Jesus Christ, Thy Son our Lord, *Amen.*

ROBERT D. HERSHEY, *The Evangelical Lutheran Church of the Holy Trinity, New York*

FOR THE THIRD SUNDAY IN NOVEMBER

LORD God of Hosts: Fountain of being: Creator and Sustainer of the Universe: we, who after the flesh are weak and of short stay, come nevertheless with boldness before Thee, and call upon Thee in confidence of Thy favour and mercy. For Thou hast given us to see in Christ that we are Thine offspring, secured against the chance and change of time by Thine eternal goodness. Acknowledging and glorifying Thine ineffable majesty, we praise Thee above all for Thy lovingkindness. We deplore our sins and folly. We beseech Thee to pardon all our shortcomings. We earnestly purpose to live henceforth in harmony with Thy will, putting behind us whatever is displeasing in Thy sight. And we invoke the support of Thy Holy Spirit, that we may be ever mindful of this resolve and may be made strong to perform it.

Thou art so great, O Lord, as to have time and care even for little things; Thou knowest all our troubles, our temptations, our griefs, our doubts. Give us Thy comfort, healing and aid; help us to be patient and courageous, and to put aside our own cares in kindness and concern for others. We present before Thee also the needs of our families; of our friends; and of the whole world, in which there are so many burdened with woes beyond any we have known. May all who are in peril or distress find Thee, and in Thee find deliverance and peace, through Jesus Christ our Saviour.

As we rejoice in the light of His Gospel, so we pray that it may shine to the uttermost parts of the earth. Prepare the hearts of mankind everywhere to hear and heed the message of redemption; and bless all who profess the faith of the Crucified, that the Church in all its branches may realize its worldwide unity, embrace its worldwide task, and advance to the conquest of mankind's allegiance to that Heavenly King whose gifts to His subjects are hope, joy, and freedom, now and evermore.

We seek Thy blessing also for the nations of the earth, that justice may be accomplished and peace brought to pass among all men; and especially for our country, that in this new era of her power she may lead the world creatively toward brotherhood, and that wisdom and guidance from on high may be vouchsafed to the people and all their magistrates, to keep us steady, straight and true, and bring us through with all Thine earthly children to that brighter day when war shall cease throughout the earth, and freedom be victorious.

And to Thee, from whom proceed all bounties, we ascribe all honour and praise, for Christ's sake. *Amen.*

RUSSELL H. STAFFORD, *Sometime President, the Hartford Seminary Foundation, Hartford, Connecticut*

FOR THANKSGIVING DAY

ALMIGHTY God, who art near to every seeking heart, even in those hours when it seems to us that the heavens are closed against us, hear the prayers of Thy people which in this hour arise unto Thee. We want one thing, and one thing alone, O God—the assurance that Thou art, and that Thou dost care. Through all that is done and said here this day, strengthen us in that assurance so that we may leave this place refreshed for the way, with new horizons of Thy greatness set around our transient lives, and with words of rejoicing in our hearts.

We give thanks unto Thee for the memories of our fathers who in their difficult days faced hardship and adversity, and were more than conquerors in Thy power. Stir us, who are their children, to reach out after the source of their strength, so that in these days we may be beyond the reach of cowardice and prudence which counsel caution in seeking Thy best. And wilt Thou grant unto us an inner steadiness of spirit which the perplexities and the fears of our time cannot disturb.

We make our offering of thanksgiving unto Thee, joining our voices with those of our people north and south, east and west. We give thanks unto Thee for every benefit of life; but, O God, allow us no satisfaction in them until with Christian devotion we have taken upon ourselves as our concern the want and the hunger and the insecurity of men and women and little children who suffer even in the hour of our prosperity. We give Thee thanks for our loves and for our homes, for the laughter of little children, for the peace of the eventide of life, for the encouragement and the strength that come as we share our days and our hopes with friends and loved ones. And we give thanks unto Thee too for standing beside us in our loneliness and in our sorrows. We live on Thee and by Thee, and through our deeds we would make our lives the expression of a thanks deeper than words can ever be.

Abide with us, O God, in this moving hour of worship in this place. Stir us in mind and heart so that we may seek to be worthy of those who went before us and who have made our lives and our place possible. As we reach out hands of prayer and faith, as we reach out in thought and imagination and hope, visit us with the reality of Thy presence and Thy care; prepare us for the days that will be ours, so that we may live them with courage as we seek to fulfill Thy purpose for us.

We make these prayers in the name and for the sake of Jesus Christ our Lord. *Amen.*

FREDERICK M. MEEK, *Old South Church, Boston, Massachusetts*

FOR THE FOURTH SUNDAY IN NOVEMBER

O GOD, Whose Voice is heard over the turmoil of the world, wherever men seek for truth, for justice, and for righteousness, speak to us that we may not be faint of heart but may go forward toward larger truth, fuller justice and Thy kingdom of righteousness. Speak to us through the needs of Thy world, that we may be enabled to forget ourselves in helping to bear the burdens of others. Speak to us through the lives of people who walk the way of life beside us, doing justly, loving mercy, walking humbly with Thee. Speak to us through the faith of all those who have trusted in Thee and been upheld and strengthened. Speak to us in the stillness of our own spirits, that we may know that we are shepherded by Thy care, guided by Thy wisdom, and sustained by Thy mighty power.

O God, who hast given Christ to be the light of our world, we pray that more and more all men may rejoice to walk in his light, and so find the paths of peace that lead to life abundant. Give to all leaders in government the light of Thy truth, and grace to serve Thy truth, that they may build good foundations for the life of the people who have trusted them. Pierce the darkness of ignorance that hangs over the world, that through Christ all men may know the truth which makes men free. Shed the light that heals upon all hurt and wounded souls, that in the assurance of Thy good purposes they may find comfort and wholeness of heart. Bring to an end the black night of cruelty and injustice, and let the new day dawn when all men shall serve Thee and one another in the spirit of love which is Thy gift in Christ.

O God, who art nearer to us than breathing, and nearer to those we love than we can know, hold them, wherever they may be, in the hollow of Thy hand, that no evil may touch their life that is hid with Christ in Thee. Enable them to meet changes of fortune with courage; to be calm in times of testing; in sickness to find health in Thee; in the hour of temptation to be strong in Thy Spirit; and at all times to be found faithful to Thee, our Lord and our God.

O God who wouldst have Thy will done on earth as it is in heaven, fill all the ways of the earth with the spirit of Thy heaven, until in Thee our world finds peace, our hearts find rest, and through every shadow that is cast by sin shines the everlasting light of Christ who taught us when we pray to say,

(Here follows an offering of the Lord's Prayer by the minister and the congregation in unison.)

MORGAN PHELPS NOYES, *Pastor Emeritus,*
Central Presbyterian Church, Montclair, New Jersey

ALMIGHTY God, we Thy people and the sheep of Thy pasture do now draw near unto Thee in reverence and godly fear. Look down upon us, we beseech Thee, and bless us. For this is none other but the house of God and the gate of heaven.

We look unto Thee and never look in vain. Thou art the Giver of every good and perfect gift. May each of Thy children here assembled receive that special blessing of which he may be in need. If any are conscious of carelessness or indifference, kindle within them a new and holy purpose to be good soldiers of our Lord Jesus Christ; if any are embittered by grief or disappointment, if sorrow has hardened or doubt has darkened their hearts, draw Thou near in Thy gentleness and pour the oil of Thy healing into any wounds their souls may bear. Grant to the penitent the sense of Thy pardon. If any have cause for special thanksgiving, may they place the gift of their gratitude upon Thine altar now.

Together with all Thy faithful people in all the world, as we begin the solemn season which celebrates the Advent of our Saviour Christ who took upon Him our human flesh, we adore Thee that Thou didst have pity upon our poor humanity and didst reveal Thyself in Him that we might know the fullness of Thy love, be assured of Thy forgiveness and of our redemption from death unto eternal life. Before the Day of His blessed nativity, may we contemplate this mystery and miracle of Grace and prepare ourselves worthily to receive Him as our Redeemer. With loving hearts we bless Thee for the peace He brings, for the good will He teaches sinful men. From the sickness of sin and the darkness of doubt; from selfish pleasures and sullen pains; from vainglory, hypocrisy and all uncharitableness, good Lord, deliver us. May we watch and pray, for in an hour that we know not the Son of Man cometh.

We praise Thee, O Lord, for the blessed Hope that His

Advent has brought into this sinful, struggling world. For He is King of Kings and Lord of Lords. All things Thou hast put under His feet and He shall reign forever and ever. In the darkest hour, when confusion and discord tempt us to despair, we remember that He is the Incarnation not only of Love, but also of Power and Might and that the travail of His soul shall not be satisfied until the kingdom of this world is become the kingdom of our Lord and of His Christ. Grant us, we beseech Thee, that through the help of His Power we may overcome all evils that oppose us and obtain the victory.

Send us on our way and may it be Thy way. May we take up our daily duties with fresh heart and courage; face our difficulties and bear our burdens, remembering Him who said, "I am with you alway, even unto the end."

Hear these our prayers according to the abundance of Thy mercy, and to Thy name be glory and power both now and forever. *Amen.*

RAYMOND CALKINS, *Pastor Emeritus,*
First Congregational Church, Cambridge, Massachusetts

FOR THE SECOND SUNDAY IN ADVENT

HOLY, Holy, Holy, Lord God Almighty, whose throne is eternal in the heavens and whose kingdom is in the hearts of men, we humbly beseech thee to accept the offering of our adoration and thankgiving and to hear our prayers as we come before thee now in penitence and faith. As of old thou gavest it to seers to see, and to prophets to speak of, the coming of thy kingdom in the earth, so do thou, of thy mercy, grant it to us to see the day of thy kingdom dawn and the shadows of sin and evil flee away.

And, that our prayer may be sincere, do thou first become Lord in our own lives. Help us to surrender all that is hindering thy reign in us and the doing of thy will through us.

We pray that thy kingdom may come in our homes, in the places where we work, in social and business relationships, in relations between management and labor, in our city councils and in our state and national legislatures. May thy Holy Spirit so inspire our minds and enlarge our hearts, that we all may be one in desire and aim to achieve a life-in-community that is in accordance with thy will.

And, as we draw near the time of the birthday of the Prince of Peace, especially do we pray that all the peoples and nations of the earth may be led into the way and the bond of peace. Let that divine, incarnate humility replace the pride and arrogance and ambition of men which make for war, and bring to us all the spirit of goodwill and of service for one another.

Give us the will, O God; the will to see and to do; and above all, the will to be used as agents and instruments of thy kingdom.

For the kingdom is thine, and the power and the glory. *Amen.*

Francis J. Moore, Sometime Editor of The Forward Movement

FOR THE THIRD SUNDAY IN ADVENT

Eternal and ever-blessed God, who in the fullness of time didst send forth Thy Son to be the Saviour of the world, lay Thy Hand upon our hearts that we may be prepared to worship Thee. Thou didst cause light to shine out of darkness through the coming of Thy Son. Let the light of Christ search our souls and scatter our darkness, separating between good and evil. May the light of his Truth expose the shadows cast by the false choices to which we have clung. May the light of his compassion be turned upon any dark moods of vengeance which we have harbored. May the light of his concern for others reveal the indifference which we have felt toward those in need.

Make these Advent days more meaningful to us. In quietness and confidence we would open the door that Christ may enter and dwell in our souls. Breathe into our hearts a rich measure of the Christ-spirit, that we may be *led* to Thee in trust and obedience and may touch the lives of all Thy children with brotherly love and sympathy.

We bring our wills to Christ, to be strengthened until our purposes are undergirded by his purpose. We bring our minds, open and receptive to his truth, that we may know that freedom whereby Christ doth set men free. We bring our hearts to be quickened, until our love meets and mingles with his love, that they may become a kingdom wherein we may walk in great places. So may our souls reflect some measure of his way, his truth and his life.

O Thou Giver of every good and perfect gift, we praise Thee for every manifestation of Thy love in Christ. In him Thou hast unveiled to the world the glory of our nature and life, and blessed the families of the earth. We thank Thee for home and childhood and for the ever-deepening bonds of friendship. Soften and fill our hearts with love and gratitude, with tenderness and peace. Consecrate our joy throughout these coming days.

We would remember, in our prayer, those for whom these days bring quickened memories of loved ones who have now gone from our earthly fellowship. We pray for those for whom these days bring extra burdens. Before Thee we would remember those whose strength is drained through extra hours of work; those whose souls may miss the joy of unselfish giving; and those who find themselves unable to give what they wish they could. Be near those who are sick and in pain; the discouraged and the fearful; the lonely and the bereaved. Touch their souls with the spirit of him who came that all men might have a more abundant life. In his Name we pray. *Amen.*

WALLACE W. ANDERSON,
United Congregational Church, Bridgeport, Connecticut

FOR THE SUNDAY BEFORE CHRISTMAS

OUR Lord and God, who in the person of Thy Son didst come to earth accompanied by songs of heaven: Help us, as we approach the anniversary of His birth, so to open our lives to Him as to be made exceeding glad, and so to yield to Him our wills as to be made surpassing strong; that we, receiving Him in our souls and obeying Him in our daily deeds, may cause many a mirthless heart to welcome Him with gladness and thanksgiving.

God of pity, whose eyes are ever upon Thy children: We thank Thee for Thy love that loved us into being, and for Thy care that seeks to keep and guide us, to pardon and restore us to Thy fellowship, and to lighten every darkened place. Especially we praise Thee for Thy mercy made manifest in Him who took upon Himself our flesh and lived among us, sharing our burden, tasting our pain and grief, bringing Thee near, turning our faces to Thy face. Enable us, we beseech Thee, so to dwell in Him, and He in us, that we may follow in His steps, and become Thy sons in spirit and in truth.

O God, whose ears are open to the cry of the penitent, and who givest grace exceeding our default: Hear us as we confess our sins. We have forgotten Thee; we have neglected our high calling in Christ Jesus; we have lived in the weakness of our own strength, and in the darkness of our own wisdom, and we have turned away from Thy strength, which in weakness is made perfect, and from Thy living Word, which makes the simple wise. But Thou, O Lord, art eager to have mercy, and to pardon, and to lift upon us the light of Thy countenance. Save us, we beseech Thee, from all our sins; redeem our days in the midst of failure; and guard us in the moment of success; that we, delivered alike from evil and from folly, may serve Thee faithfully in joyfulness and love.

Almighty and ever-living God, who hast made Thy Church the cradle of Christ and the abiding home of His Spirit: Confirm in her behalf Thine ancient promises, and, in this present time, restore her soul; that she, persuaded by Thine indwelling presence, and emboldened by Thy besetting guard, may put aside timidity and every sinful hindrance, and may show forth, in worship and in life, the mind and might of Jesus Christ her Lord.

Father of all mankind: Come with the shining of Thy comfort to every frightened child of Thine who cries upon Thee; bestow on each, according to his need, Thy gracious gifts. Guide the wanderer; cheer the lonely; speak to the disordered mind Thy word of peace; encourage those who are weighted and bound by chains of desire, and mercifully set them free in the holy bondage of Christ; and, through Thy fellowship in suffering, draw Thou the sting of every earthly hurt.

God of the nations: Be with all the nations, though they be not with Thee; and lead mankind into newness of purpose and of patience, until peace with righteousness shall reign.

Grant, O Lord, that those things which, without Thee, we

cannot accomplish, may be brought within and through us by Thy Spirit; and that those things which, apart from us, Thou canst not bring to pass, may find fulfillment in our willingness to do Thy will; for the sake of Jesus Christ our Lord. *Amen.*

JOHN UNDERWOOD STEPHENS
*Former Minister of the Mount Washington
Presbyterian Church, New York City*

FOR THE LAST SUNDAY OF THE YEAR

ALMIGHTY God, our King and Lawgiver, again we come to thee in prayer. We call upon thee in thy might who hast made the earth and ordained our lives. We call upon thee in thy mercy, by whom the dayspring from on high has visited us. We call upon thee in the hymn of the morning stars, of all creatures, of angels and archangels and all the company of heaven, saying, "Holy, holy, holy, Lord God of hosts, heaven and earth are full of thy glory."

O Lord of power and grace, we bring thee our thanksgivings for thy mercies unto us.

We thank thee for the echoes of Christmas carols and happy voices, for the angel-song which still lingers about us. We thank thee for our greatest gift, the vision ever new of thy revelation to us in a manger, where heaven touches earth and we are saved.

We thank thee for the year which so soon comes to its close.

For twelve months of thine unfailing mercies,

We thank thee, heavenly Father.

For seedtime and harvest, summer and winter, for sun and rain, darkness and light,

We thank thee, heavenly Father.

For daily bread and nightly rest, for loads to lift and lives to love,

We thank thee, heavenly Father.

For thy power in our days of strength and thy mercy in our days of weakness,

We thank thee, heavenly Father.

For whatever our nation has done which endures to thy glory, for whatever hopes and dreams of mankind that have been brought even one step closer to this waiting world,

We thank thee, heavenly Father, and praise and glorify thy holy name.

Dear Lord, our father and our judge, as the year ends we confess unto thee our sins. Our circling year has been too much another march around the ringed ruts of ancient customs. The easy roads have all been worn further down. We have neither looked up far enough, nor served men long enough. We have not trusted thee enough in living faith. And yet during this same year we have busied ourselves on our own behalf. We have cried, "What shall we eat, what shall we drink, and wherewithal shall we be clothed?" Spare us these our faults, our very grievous faults. As the old year gives way to the new, let us lift up our hearts to thy forgiving love. Let the weight of our former lives be not held against us, but rather may we be renewed as thy sons and daughters for another year of grace.

O God of the human brotherhood, as we stand at the door of the old year, we pray thy blessing upon all who have touched our lives. Be with those who have been our familiar friends in the year past, that our familiarity may not wear away their knowledge of their worth to us. Be with our unseen friends who have lighted and lightened our lives when we knew it not. Guard the magistrates of our land and all lands, O thou who art the God of all. Lead those who have sought the paths of darkness and evil into the saving joy of thy light and love. From our several paths wherein we have strayed, lead us into the single upward way of truth.

And now, as in thy grace we step toward another year, we pray, O Lord, that thou be with us.

Let thy pillar of cloud or fire be our sufficient guide.

Let us seek thy will in all joy or pain.

Let us seek thy love in hours of exultation and days of sorrow.

Let us seek thy kingdom in every effort of our crowded lives, that the heartbeat of this earthly stay may be sustained to thy glory.

So may the year to come begin in the new grace of the season now to close and rise in our strengthened wills. May it shine among men as a time of the power of the Holy Spirit.

Keep us ever in thy loving care, and may the year to come bring us twelve months nearer to our fulfilment as men and to our eternal home in thee.

Through Jesus Christ, thy son, our Lord, we have offered this our morning prayer. *Amen.*

ROBERT L. EDDY
*The United Congregational Church,
Little Compton, Rhode Island*

OTHER SPECIAL PRAYERS

FOR THE ANNIVERSARY
OF A LOCAL CHURCH—I

O GOD, who art the Inspiration of all that is good, the Support of all faithful men, and the Reward of all those that seek Thy face,

Enrich our thanksgiving this day with the benediction of Thy spirit. Help us to draw new courage for the future from the story of Thy Providence in the past. Enable us to garner from the experience of days gone the wisdom that we need for the unknown days ahead. Strengthen in our midst the influence of every good tradition. Give us clear judgment to discern that which is eternally true from that which is temporary and outworn, that we may prove all things, and hold fast to that which is good. With gratitude for all that has been, and aware of that which can never be taken from us, may we set our faces forward, ready for new endeavors, eager for new experiences of Thy grace, and utterly consecrated to Thy service.

O God, who hast set us in days of confusion, turmoil and strife, hearten us, we beseech Thee, with the memory of stalwart men who in other days of trial have served Thee unafraid and unashamed. Help us to meet the needs of our time with like courage and like devotion. Remind us afresh of Thy supreme gift to earth in the life and spirit of the Man of Galilee, and help us to find the answers to all our problems in his clear mind and in his friendly heart. Bind us in fellowship with his ambassadors in all the earth, and give us grace never to be discouraged and never to cease from high endeavor until all men call him Lord, and our troubled, sinful world becomes the kingdom of his love.

O God of life eternal, lift us this day into new fellowship of spirit with the church triumphant, the good company of those who have fought the good fight, finished their course, and kept the faith. Make our thought of them bright with the Christian hope, and make our life here so true to their hopes for us that no failure of ours could ever cause them shame or sorrow. Bring us all at last into the closer fellowship of the realms of light, where Christ is, where our beloved are with him, and where we too one day would be. *Amen.*

Morgan Phelps Noyes, *Pastor Emeritus,*
Central Presbyterian Church, Montclair, New Jersey

FOR THE ANNIVERSARY
OF A LOCAL CHURCH—II

O God, who art the same yesterday, today, and forever, we beseech Thee to empower with Thy spirit this church, over whose hundred years Thou hast watched. We bless Thee for those who first banded themselves together on this mountainside to be a church of Christ; for Thy Providence guiding and guarding this fellowship these many years; for all who have ministered here in Thy name; for those who have gone out from this, their home church, to preach the gospel by word and by life in other places; for all the lives that have been dedicated here to Thy service; for all who have found comfort here in the everlasting presence; for every influence that has gone out from this church to strengthen and uplift this community and the wider world of which it is a part.

Confirm now in us the faith by which the fathers have here worshipped and served Thee. Open our eyes, that we may see the new tasks which Thou hast waiting for our hands, and give us hearts and hands ready for the tasks. Enlarge our sympathies, that no human need may find us unresponsive, and that in the eyes of every needy brother we may see the light of Christ.

Quicken our consciences, that we may know what is His will for us in this new day, and give us courage to do the right as Thou givest us to see the right. Remind us that as Thou hast led Thy people through many a wilderness, so Thou art able to be our Deliverer in this perplexing time, and to make us more than conquerors through him who loved us and gave himself for us.

Company this day with all whose thoughts are toward this house of prayer, and make us one fellowship through Thy spirit dwelling with us. We ask for our loved ones in distant places every good gift of Thy love. Shine with the light of Thy friendly countenance upon all whom this day finds in illness or in pain. Comfort with the healing of the everlasting hope those in any sorrow. Strengthen and encourage those who have met disappointment or any loss. Make us one company in faith and in triumphant life.

Eternal God, Lord of every world, before whom stand the spirits of the living and the dead; we bless Thy name for all Thy servants departed this life in Thy faith and fear; and especially for those most dear to us; and we beseech Thee to give us grace so to follow their good example that even here we may be united with them in fellowship of spirit; and that finally when we too are called hence, we may be gathered with them in the everlasting light and peace. *Amen.*

MORGAN PHELPS NOYES, *Pastor Emeritus,*
Central Presbyterian Church, Montclair, New Jersey

AT A RELIGIOUS WORKERS' CONFERENCE

ALMIGHTY and Eternal Father, from whom alone comes the true counsel of our hearts: grant to us now the full shining of Thy countenance that no darkness may cloud our understanding, or any earthly feeling move us from Thy will. We rejoice in Thy truth as the assurance of our deliverance. We are strong and ready when we remember Thy ways, to do them. We are confident as we feel the presence of Thy Spirit upon us, even as a father's hand to guide and uphold. Make us to feel now in the quiet of this hour that though the earth should change and the mountains shake in the heart of the sea, that the Rock of our salvation is sure and shall not be moved.

As Thou hast committed to us the mystery of Thy Grace through the ministry of Thy blessed Son, and caused us to dwell in the fellowship of His Church, make us to be faithful witnesses of all Thou hast revealed. Let no vain fondness deter our errand. Keep us back from presumptuous sins. Deliver us from all folly of mind or flesh, that those who look up to us may find light and leading and healing.

In all the varying voices that are heard through the din and strife of our distressed age, we would be sensitive instruments to catch the assurance of Thy calling, and echo it to a weary and waiting world.

Forgive our foolish ways, we humbly beseech Thee, and lighten our present path by the calm and steadfast faith in Him who became for us and for all men the Way of Life Everlasting. *Amen.*

WOFFORD C. TIMMONS, *Sometime Director,*
Congregational Commission on Evangelism;
Late Pastor, Church of the Wide Fellowship,
Southern Pines, North Carolina

FOR THE WORLD OF MEN

Four short pastoral prayers each to be offered in a service in addition to other, special prayers to be given at various points in the service.

I.

O GOD, who art the provider and sustainer of our life, we here acknowledge thy over-ruling providence which shapes our ends, rough-hew them how we will. We thank thee for our faith that by thy greatness round about our littleness, more can be done with human instruments than we can ask or think. Make us ever more grateful that thy power is never absent but is always hidden in events, forever prompting men to do the best things in the worst times, and making the darkest days the times of revelation. And grant us in all our doubts and uncertainties a conscience undimmed by the narrowness of pious men, that we may be worthy of the unapplauded sacrifice of those who watched over our thoughtless years, through Jesus Christ our Lord. *Amen.*

II.

MOST merciful Father, we who have all fallen short do here humbly confess our pretended self-sufficiency that holds not thee in awe; that we may be on guard against the knowledge that stores our minds without opening our hearts, and the skill that gives power without wisdom, lest we take unwitting part in man's inhumanity to man. From the pride of race or class that would prevent our service to those who need most what we enjoy; from the temptations of greed that draw men after one another in the fever of covetous quest to confound the purpose of our creator; and from narrow pride in outworn ways and blind eyes that see no need of change, Good Lord, deliver us, through Jesus Christ our Lord. *Amen.*

III.

O THOU Giver of life, by whose spirit our life may be renewed day by day, since we pass this way but once, keep us sure that our peculiar self is an agent of thy great creation. Hold us to those duties which are dearer than life itself, that through all loneliness and disappointment and all the troubles that beset us we may still have that to which we give ourselves away, fearing only to be unfaithful and having no other fear. *Amen.*

IV.

GOD of our Fathers and our God, enlighten by thy spirit those who lead our people in confusing times, and help us as a nation to preserve for the whole human race the heritage that outlives the riches of this world. Raise up among us those who stand ready for the thoughts that will rule the future, and who fear no destruction that clears a way through man's obstinate desire to be undisturbed. And grant above all that, for the sake of all men, we may in our home and school and church nurture a continuing company who know no lord save the Lord our God, and who will be citizens first of thy kingdom, resolved to be more thine than their country's or their own. Once more confirm our devotion to the significance of each individual man, responsible to his people and to thee, that a few may do by their excellence what a crowd cannot do by its strength.

This as all our prayers we make in the name of our Lord and Savior Jesus Christ. *Amen.*

ROBERT RUSSELL WICKS
Dean of the Chapel, Emeritus,
Princeton University

FOR ANY NEW BEGINNING

O LORD our God, we give Thee hearty thanks for a Gospel which proclaims this the year of the Lord's favor; this, the day when Thy salvation and help are given. For One who goeth before us in the way, even for Him who is the Shepherd of our souls, we bless Thee. As He knoweth them that are His and leadeth them forth, grant to us willing and trusting hearts to follow where He leads now and evermore.

Our Father, for all our past neglect of Thy light and leading, and for all our refusal of a strength and help ready to hand, do Thou grant us now forgiveness, even as we pray for the gift of Thy grace to the end that what we see we may do; that what we know to be right and just we may perform in the spirit of Jesus.

Renew before our face, we pray Thee, the vision of Thy distant goals which are the end of all our journeying. Give us the vision of the grace of God which hath measured our lot and hath matched itself against our needs with promise to make us more than conquerors. Give us remembrance of the comradeship of Christ which knows no east nor west, north nor south, bond nor free, but only one great brotherhood of love throughout the whole wide earth. Give us sight of the kingdom of righteousness, justice and truth whose wealth is neither silver nor gold, whose law is love, whose end is the building of all men into the image of Christ.

As Thou dost renew the vision, so make plain the way, the roads to take and travel: the way of brother-keeping, the way of good will, the way of forgiveness, the way of prayer and the way of obedience until all things in us and in our world find their fulfillment in Thee through Jesus Christ our Lord, *Amen.*

FREDERICK W. ALDEN, *Minister to the*
New Hampshire Congregational Conference

A PRAYER TO ACCOMPANY A SERMON
on "THE GOD THAT WORKS"

My Father is working still, and I work.
—JOHN 5:17

OUR Father, we thank thee that we may enter thy presence again as a worshipping congregation. We lift our hearts to thee in praise and adoration. Thou art the Holy One, far above us in glory and goodness and might. But thou hast made us for thyself and thou dost draw near to us in love and mercy. Be with us in the worship of this hour. Grant us thy Spirit that we may hear thy word and know thee, that we may come before thee in humility and reverence and trust.

We thank thee, O Father, for him whom thou didst send, for thy Son, our Lord and Savior. We praise thee for him who died for us and whom thou didst raise from the dead. We thank thee that in him we know thy forgiving mercy. In penitence we confess to thee our sins. We have followed too much the desires of our own hearts. We have done the things that we should not have done and have left undone what we should have done. Forgive us and grant us grace to do thy will.

We thank thee that in Jesus thou hast shown us the way of life. Help us to walk in that way. Guide, we pray thee, the leaders of the nations. We thank thee that they are seeing more and more that only as they take his way of freedom and justice and good will can the peoples of this earth escape destruction and find prosperity and peace. We thank thee for the rich blessings which thou hast bestowed upon this land of ours. Help us to see that these are a trust from thee. Help us to use them in the service of the many that are in need and to work with others that peace may come upon earth.

We thank thee, our Father, for the kingdom of God that is here and for the kingdom that is to come. May the hope of that coming kingdom strengthen our hearts. May our hearts take courage because we know that thou art with us and that thou art working in the world. May we face the world of evil with confidence, knowing that he that is with us is greater than all the forces of evil.

We thank thee for thy church, for the body of Christ in which he dwells and through which he works. We thank thee that in thy mercy thou hast received us into this family of thy children. Be thou our strength. Help us to come to thee in worship, knowing that thou art here with us. We praise thee as we remember all thy mercies. Help us to open our hearts to thee, confessing our sins, trusting in thy forgiving love, receiving thy Spirit.

We pray for the church universal, the fellowship of thy people throughout the earth. We thank thee that we belong to this worldwide church. May we remember it in our prayers, sustain it with our gifts, and seek to carry thy gospel to the lands that lie in darkness. We pray for a deeper unity among the many churches which own a common Lord and hold a common faith. Heal our divisions. Unite thy children here in this land and throughout the world. Bring us into a rich and vital fellowship so that we may bear a clearer witness and better do thy work.

We thank thee, Father, for the kingdom that is to come, here on earth, and in the life beyond. We know that neither life nor death can separate us from the love of God. Our fellowship with thee and with thy people is an eternal one. We thank thee that death itself is but the open door through which we pass to join the eternal household of our God where there is no death or separation. Keep us faithful to thee and receive us at last into thy kingdom above to join those who have gone before. And thine shall be the praise and the glory, world without end. We pray in Jesus' name. *Amen.*

HARRIS FRANKLIN RALL, *Professor Emeritus,*
Garrett Biblical Institute,
Evanston, Illinois

A PRAYER OF THANKSGIVING
IN TIMES OF DISTRESS

O ALMIGHTY God, whom we dare approach because thy judgment upon us is always encompassed about by thy mercy toward us, we give thee thanks for thy forgiving love, offered to us at the point of our deepest need and insufficiency, and assured us by the life and death and rising again of thy Son Jesus Christ our Lord.

We thank thee that in the midst of the blackest moments of our lives we need not be alone, since thou art always with us, and as close to us as we will let thee be. We thank thee that in thy Son thou hast shared and entered into our feelings of dereliction and forsakenness. Help us, at those moments when we too cry "My God, My God, why hast thou forsaken me?" to be able also by thy grace to breathe forth in utter trust, "Father, into thy hands I commit my spirit."

We thank thee that in the midst of the great mysteries of life—of birth, of death, of love, of sorrow, of grace—we do not face only mystery, but find meaning in the midst of mystery, as we look through a glass darkly and find not only darkness but also, shining through the darkness, the light of the knowledge of the glory of God in the face of Jesus Christ.

We thank thee that in the midst of self-contempt, unworthiness and sin we do not find condemnation piled upon condemnation, but the faithful promise that if we confess our sin thou art faithful and just to forgive us our sin and to cleanse us from all unrighteousness, a promise which we know to be the truth as we see it in the very life and death of one who says "I am the truth."

We thank thee that thou hast not condemned us to live isolated and lonely lives, but that thou hast placed us in communities of persons, to whom we can open ourselves, with whom we can share, in whom we can trust, and by whom we can be accepted. Help us to know that thy divine love and concern can touch us through human love and concern, and that human love and concern can be sacramental of thy divine love and concern.

We thank thee that in the midst of our incomplete and broken lives, thou dost come to us in a life that is complete and full and whole, not only showing us a more excellent way, but offering us thy grace as we falteringly try to walk that way which Christ hath shown us.

We thank thee for thy church, and for the way in which it can be a true community of grace, where love and acceptance and forgiveness are real, and where spite and censoriousness and hypocrisy are rooted out by the power of thy Spirit. We thank thee that thy church embraces the whole company of the faithful, across all time and space, so that the praise we render thee on earth is but a pale reflection of the praise continually rendered thee in heaven. May we, then, in company with all the faithful both in heaven and on earth, continually offer up our words and our deeds and our lives—and our distresses—as a sacrifice of praise and thanksgiving unto thee, to whom be all honor and glory, both now and forever more. *Amen.*

Robert McAfee Brown
Union Theological Seminary, New York

FOR A LAYMEN'S SUNDAY

A Prayer Such as a Layman Might Offer

Almighty God, we come to seek thy presence here today. Our hearts have praised thy name in joyful song. Here in thy house we recall thine ancient mercies. Here is our joy of earth and our hope of heaven.

We confess unto thee, dear Lord, our many shortcomings

in the week past. As we think back over it we remember how we have fallen short in thought and word and deed. We have thought too much about ourselves. We have spoken hastily and with too little charity. We have labored largely for a greater share of this world's goods and we have forgotten to seek thy kingdom and its righteousness first, that all else needful might be added unto us of thy bounty and care. Forgive us, we pray, these and all our other faults in thy fatherly love. Take us by our humility and lift us to a better self in which we may live in closer company with thee and listen more closely for thy will and word for us.

Dear Heavenly Father, we pray this morning for all men. Be with worshipers near and far who call upon thee in varied tongue and song. Look with love upon men of all colors and all honest vocations. Grant thy protection and wisdom to the President of the United States, and all guardians and servants of the public trust. Keep in thy care the men of the armed services, that though they take the wings of the morning and dwell in the uttermost parts of the sea, even there thy hand may lead them and thy right hand may hold them. Look with light and mercy upon any who may live in bondage to sin or in the oppression of any of their neighbors. Speed the day when all the tools of war shall be melted in the triumph of wise men of good will. Let thy kingdom come, and thy will be done, beginning with us here before thee now.

We ask for ourselves that thou give us strength. We ask for strength to earn our daily bread, but ask thee more for the hidden strength which overcomes the world. Touch our lives by thy Spirit, that as workmen in store and office, shop and field, we may do our work for thee. Let us so labor each day that at evening we may offer up our day's work as an adornment of thy earth or as a service to our fellow-men. We ask also for strength to do the right, without wavering under thy watchful and loving eye. Let us in the power of this moment keep true to its vision of the world that is to be when all life is led in the very fellowship of this hour.

And, lastly, we ask thy peace upon us. Keep our hearts from fretting over the ways of this world. Let us drink here the draughts of silence which set at naught the distractions of the world without. Let thy will for us be our peace, as we resign ourselves to the call of thy word. And may this peace be our sufficient reward as thy children and workmen until the day is done and our spirits rise to rest forever with thee. Be with us and our loved ones all the week long, and hear us when we pray, calling unto thee ever as now in the name of our Lord and saviour Jesus Christ. *Amen.*

ROBERT L. EDDY,
United Congregational Church,
Little Compton, Rhode Island

FOR A YOUTH SUNDAY

or A BOY SCOUT SUNDAY

ALMIGHTY God, with joyful hearts we come to praise thy name. We hail thee in the beauties of the world 'round about us. In the treasures of the snow and the clothing of the lilies thy wonder is past our understanding. We love thee as our creator, who hast given us dominion over the beast of the field, who hast made us but a little lower than the angels and hast crowned us with glory and honor. But most of all we praise thee for thy son our Lord Jesus Christ who by his life and death showed us the way to life and thee. All that is within us would praise thy holy name.

Wash away, we ask, our sins and imperfections of the week past. Forgive us our smallness of heart, our fear to turn the other cheek, our grudgingness in offering our coat to our neighbor in need. Awaken our eyes to the world about us yet unborn to us, prepare us to meet the great work before us which awaits our hands and heads and hearts. Give us a newness of spirit that we may rise up and fare forth into new lands of living unto new goals of loving.

We pray this morning for all thy children about the world. Look with love upon men in all lands who turn their eyes to thee, who bare their hearts to thy sustaining mercy. Bless, we pray thee, the President of the United States, and all who serve under our flag, that their minds may be inspired by thy wisdom and their hearts sustained by thy power, to the end that our beloved country may thrive and grow as one of the world's best hopes of the brotherhood of all peoples.

We pray this morning for these young people here before thee. In thy sight we know how soon they will be our workers, our leaders, our rulers. We are reminded here how short are the years in which they are to become endowed with every good grace and gift to fight manfully in all thy battles. Grant that they may be strong and increase in the glow of health. Save them from habits that harm. Lead them to know the ironclad laws of self-care, that their lives may be led in calm and sturdy frames.

Grant that they may be awake in mind. Lead them to the treasures of wisdom and lore in the past. Inspire them with heroes' tales. And so teach them to apply the wisdom of their schooling to the many crossroads of life that their wisdom and grace may bear them safely. Grant that they may early seek and find the straight road of the right, and that, with thy whole armor put on, they may pursue the right road, and serve in the cause of the good life unto the end.

Almighty God, whose Son Jesus Christ did as a youth grow

in wisdom and stature and in favor with men and thee, we pray this manifold blessing for our youth, that, as the swiftly coming soldiers and builders of his kingdom, they may be wanting in no good thing, but by thy grace may live lives as men indeed in Christ's company and in the end win through him life everlasting. In his name and for his sake we have asked this our morning prayer. *Amen.*

ROBERT L. EDDY,
United Congregational Church,
Little Compton, Rhode Island

GENERAL PASTORAL PRAYERS

OUR Father, who hast called us to returning and rest, in these moments of prayer we hear at last and we heed. We come in awe and reverence because in Thee is both majesty and mystery. Who can know Thee? Yet, we do know Thee, for Thou hast disclosed Thyself even in the common bush afire to catch our eye. Thou hast come as close as the bread we break and the cup we take that none shall miss Thee. Thou hast even humbled Thyself until the Word has become flesh and dwelt among us.

We are deeply moved to make our confession. Hear us as Thou hast promised. Some of us have come to this very hour deep in the anguish of remorse, for our sins have been grievous. We have violated all we held decent and true. There is no health for us but in Thy grace and no freedom but in Thy forgiveness. Some of us have sinned not in an hour of tempestuous temptation but in the careless dropping of our integrity, a little at a time, in moments that became days and days that became weeks until our lives have become bound and tedious and drab. Is this, too, Thy divine judgment? Then, grant us Thy forgiveness that we may be made right again.

We would not pray for ourselves alone. So many of us face this day in the darkness of despair, in anguish or pain, with their souls in crisis. They wait in fear, even in the shadow of death. Others are in frantic flight from Thee, from the one encounter which could make their lives whole and fair. They flee in a mist of tears or under that running laughter which is hollow and frantic. O seeking, brooding Spirit of God, who dost bring healing in Thy hands and dost redeem by Thy love, we pray for all these who with us need Thee so much.

In this week we would trust Thee all the day long and with all that we are. Let our minds trust Thee that they may know tranquility. Let our bodies trust Thee that they may know health. Let our wills trust Thee that we may have singleness of heart. Let our emotions trust Thee that even under the stress of the day we may know inner harmony and at eventide come to serenity. Let our work trust Thee that it may be worthy and honorable. Let our love trust Thee that it may be mature and free. So, may we know the word of the Psalmist, "Bless the Lord, O my soul, and all that is within me," through Jesus Christ, our Lord. *Amen.*

GENE E. BARTLETT, *First Baptist Church,*
Los Angeles, California

FOR ALL NATIONS

ALMIGHTY God our Father, we glorify Thy name because Thou art great and holy, dwelling in the midst of light our eyes cannot penetrate. We give Thee praise that may not be uttered that Thou hast not suffered Thyself to be contained even in that light and that out of love (which is Thine own proper nature) Thy spirit has overflowed its limits and gone out to all the earth. Who are we that we should make our voice heard in the place where Thy glory dwelleth? Who are we that in our imperfection and dereliction we should deserve Thy mercy or even Thy justice? But Thou, O Lord, hast made it known to us that Thy compassion does not wait upon our merit: it is Thou who comest to us, as we cannot come to Thee. We should not love Thee, hadst Thou not already loved us, and revealed to us the meaning and power of Thy love.

Let Thy blessing, we humbly pray, be upon all whom we bless in Thy name. Spare the nations from each other, that they may learn to live as one people in mutual understanding, their rivalries turned to emulations for the public good, their arts bringing them to united sympathies and hopes, their science become the ingenuity of love. Look with especial mercy upon those who are called by the warring of the nations into places of great danger: the soldiers and sailors, the airmen and civilians whose lives are jeopardized by the blind hate which, if suffered, grows up along national boundaries.

Help us all to remember that it is the way of redemption that those who will follow Thee shall take upon themselves the guilt of the guilty. We do not separate ourselves from those who sin against Thee: we are one family, and as a priesthood for Thy people now ask Thy forgiveness, begging for a vision of the better way and the courage to walk in it. *Amen.*

DOUGLAS HORTON
*Dean of Harvard Divinity School,
Cambridge, Massachusetts*

FOR FAITH AND PEACE:
A PRAYER IN OUR OWN WORDS*

THANK You, Lord Christ, for all who have been healed in any way through their Christian faith. Their experience, their suffering and their triumph have increased our faith and made us ashamed of ourselves. It has also made us determined that hereafter we shall not allow ourselves to be defeated by fear. We have been afraid and therefore we hid our talent in a napkin instead of using it for Thy glory. Help us to go out of here to-

* Pages 27-29 of "How to Pray Today," a pamphlet published by Mothers of the World, Incorporated, Oklahoma City, Oklahoma. Offered for this book by Dr. Laubach, and adapted for use as a general pastoral prayer by the editor.

day unafraid of anything or anybody. We need not be afraid of any person in the world, because nobody can hurt us. We need to fear only to let go of Thy hand. May we from this day on, all of us, keep closer and closer, and every day learn better and better what it means to be the intimate friend of the Lord Jesus Christ. Having Thee by our side, having Thee whisper within us, so that for us to live, will be no longer ourselves alone, but the Christ who lives in us.

Now we pray Thee for these men who are struggling in the United Nations to find a way to peace. We pray for every one of them. God help those men while we pray, that they may pray and as they pray, they may hear Thee speak. Help them to find the God of our Lord Jesus Christ, the Father who loves like Christ and then to pray; not that they may defeat other people, but that all men everywhere, in America, in the Kremlin, may come to the feet of Jesus. We thank Thee that Thou hast told us to pray for all men, that all men may be saved. Thou didst say, "It is the will of God that all men should be saved, and come to a knowledge of the truth." So, help us all, everywhere, who call ourselves Christians, to pray for everybody. We pray Thee for the men in the Kremlin, not because that is the easiest thing to pray for, but because it is so important. Help the whole of Soviet Russia, somehow, to be able to see Jesus Christ as Paul saw Him on the way to Damascus. We know it is Thy will for them and for Russia to be saved. We pray Thee that the Russian nation may come back to Jesus Christ. Give grace to those Baptists and those others in Russia who are still loyal to Christ. Help them to be overflowing with the Spirit of Christ, so that everybody seeing them may see Him. Now we pray for our own country; our country that's putting her faith in her money, and bombs and guns and jet planes. We pray that our country may return to Christ and that we may take the Christ's way to win the world with the love of Christ; to conquer the world's heart by serving humbly. Oh what a tremendous conversion the United States has got to have right away. We pray for it. It seems to us so obvious that it would be so utterly easy to win the world's heart and to bring peace on earth, if only enough of us around the world would turn our backs on the wrong way and adopt the way of Jesus; the way of love. We pray Thee for our President and our Congressmen. May we pray often for them, and then may we write to them—telling them that we want peace on earth and good will —the Christ way of helpfulness for those who are in need. We thank Thee for this morning; we thank Thee for this church, and pray that it may keep on growing in size and spiritual power until at last the spirit that is at the heart of it, which is the Spirit of Jesus Christ, may conquer the world. Then Thy Kingdom will come and Thy will be done on earth as it is in Heaven. *Amen.*

FRANK C. LAUBACH, *Honorary President,*
World Literacy, Incorporated, New York

A NEW PRAYER FOR ALL KINDS
AND CONDITIONS OF MEN

O THOU who hast been the dwelling-place of Thy children in all generations, we who are mortal, subject to time and change, reach through our fugitive shadows to find the support of Thy enduring love, the light of Thy wisdom, and the healing of Thy mercies, according not to the measures of our deservings, but according to the measure of our need. We thank Thee for the fellowship of prayer and praise in which our meeting together is established. For the seen and the unseen whose greetings welcome us here, for the clasp of friendly hands and for the communion of the saints who from their labors rest we give Thee most humble and hearty thanks.

We praise Thee for the open doors of Thy sanctuaries across whose thresholds we find the secret of Thy grace and peace. We bless Thee for the assurances of pardon which await here those who truly repent them of their sins. Forgive us, we beseech Thee, the reproach of the evil we have done and the good undone we might have done. And grant that hereafter we may lead godly, righteous, and sober lives, and bear away with us the peace of a good conscience and the blessed light of a clearer spiritual vision.

We praise Thee for Thy mercies manifest toward us in the unfailing succession of the days, the sequence of dawns rich in promise and waiting to welcome us to new tasks. We bless Thee for the benediction of twilight when the day's work is done. We pray Thee for all our comrades in the pilgrimage of life, whatever their condition or status. Be merciful, we beseech Thee, to little children; remember them in all their needs for love and understanding, and shelter them from the hazards of a troubled world. We pray Thee for young people always and everywhere the full blessings of strength and eagerness. May they find fulfilled the promise of a happier world. Touch their dreams with power and fulfillment and keep them true to the heavenly vision.

Be with those upon whom the burdens of the Christian order are laid. Give them strength and patience, and may they see the travail of their souls and be satisfied.

Remember in the fullness of Thy mercy all those for whom the years have begun to run their course, and grant to them that at eventide it may be light.

Guide and strengthen all those who seek peace and pursue it. Bless all the efforts of those who in any fashion seek the quelling of hostilities and the realization of enduring peace.

Be with us as we make our homeward ways, and fill with a

serene happiness the waiting hours. And so make of all our days steps by which we may climb from the temporal to the enduring. In the Master's name, *Amen.*

Gaius Glenn Atkins, *Late Secretary of Evangelism in the Congregational Churches*

CONFESSION AND INTERCESSION

Almighty and most merciful Father, we come into thy presence in penitence and humility. We know that we have done what we ought not to have done and we have left undone what we ought to have done. We share the guilt of all mankind, and we seek thy forgiveness.

We ask thy forgiveness for all who are truly repentant of their sins, and we seek thy guidance for those who are unaware of their sins. Have mercy upon us, O Lord, and pardon thy transgressors.

We praise thee, O God, for thou art merciful and full of loving-kindness. Great is thy power, and thy creation serves thy will. We know that thou art with us in all that we do, sustaining us as we seek thy kingdom, and judging us when we turn from thy paths. Thou art our Father; we are the clay and thou art the potter. Bless us, O Lord. Bless us, O Lord, with thy pardon and peace.

We ask thy blessing upon this congregation. Grant to them what they need, whether they pray for it or not, and do not give them what they do not need, even though they pray for it. To each of them give what is expedient in thy sight. Bless them and their families, heal the sick, help the downtrodden, and sustain the spiritual growth of those who seek thy will.

We pray that in these times the leaders of our land may be guided by thy will and led by thy light. Keep their eyes open, their wits keen, and their judgments accurate, that they may read the signs of the times and may choose what is right. Bless especially the President of these United States, the Congress, and those in high places, that our country may be kept free from poverty, insecurity, and false promises.

In these times of stress and calamity, O Lord God, when life is hard to maintain and cheap to lose, bless the nations seeking the means of peace. Build up in all men such a love of thy Name that they will live together in brotherhood and mutual trust.

We remember the homes in which thy people dwell. Build such love between parents that security and happiness may prevail in their families, and joyous and dynamic peace may pervade their lives. Let thy grace flourish, O Lord, to heal all homes broken by discord, to comfort families in which loved ones have been lost, and to give courage to parents in the face of responsibility and travail. Bless all children and youth, that they may find acceptance, moral ideals, and freedom to grow in faith.

Grant, O God, that our minds may be guided by thy light, that we may be led in the spirit of truth to the abundant life. Grant that we may learn from those who have gone before, who have seen the light and been transformed by the light; so that in our outgoings and incomings, in our labor and in our play, in victory and in defeat, in all life and in the evening of death, we may see life steadily and see it whole. May we meet life joyously and bear its burdens with a stout heart, and may we find at the last that peace which the world cannot give, through Jesus Christ our Lord. *Amen.*

Randolph Crump Miller
Yale Divinity School,
New Haven, Connecticut

WE KNOW OURSELVES IN PRAYER

ALMIGHTY God, we worship Thee. We come knowing our need of Thee. What strange creatures we are to ourselves. We are stirred by yearnings which leave us tangled and confused; haunted by hopes which pull us in opposite ways. Knowing the tug of eternity, we yet pretend there is only earth; knowing evil is dark ruin, we yet are enamored of it; knowing our hunger for Thee, we yet flee from Thee.

Again and again before Thee we discover ourselves. What we find sometimes discourages us, sometimes frightens us, and always affirms what we have known deepest of all: that only in Thee do we find purpose that lifts our life into focus, peace that releases our potential, power that undergirds our days with assurance, and love that conquers our bent for evil.

Thou Who art the Father of all people and the Judge of nations, hear our prayer for the President of this nation and all who share responsibility of leadership with him.

Endue them with a reverent heart that they may be aware of Thee; with a humble mind that they may be led by Thee; with a pure spirit that they may be empowered by Thee.

Protect them from the pitfalls of power; from the schemes and devices of evil men; from despair at the sloth of good men.

And grant to us, the people of this nation, a new birth of righteousness, a deepened dedication to freedom and brotherhood that our country may be a refuge for truth, a hand of kindness, and a light of peace for all the earth.

This we ask in the name of Jesus Christ, King of Kings and Lord of Lords, and our Saviour. *Amen.*

EVERETT W. PALMER
The First Methodist Church,
Glendale, California

LORD God of righteousness, of justice, honor, and equity, dare we believe thy prophets and seers, men who have spoken to us with human voices, and who yet spoke in thy name? Shall we take what mere men say as thy law, thy word and thy way?

Yet if we do not listen to men, whose voice shall we hear? If we heed not men, wilt thou speak to us? Shall we hear thy voice in our inmost souls? Emblazon thy divine law upon our hearts, speak thy thoughts to conscience, touch with fire our flagging spirits.

Thou God of the earnest heart, the inquiring mind and the unlimited imagination, thou with whom dwelleth brotherhood and beauty, we ask of thee today only this—that we may believe the inmost promptings of our hearts, the utterances of our prophets and seers, mankind's ever-growing vision of loveliness and honor, mercy and understanding. Give us the faith to believe that our dreams of righteousness and peace rise from the nature of things, from the very heart of the cosmos itself. Help us to believe that the ideals for which we live and for which men down the ages have gladly died are more real than day, more eternal than time, more fundamental than life itself. Banish from us forever the lurking fear that goodness is a wisp of hope and brotherhood a convenient device, the whims and playthings of men.

O thou our God, help us to know that our visions and dreams of better things yet to be are the faint, far-off perceptions of what is. As we behold beauty, as we experience love, as we grasp truth, may we see in them thine eternity, thy totality, the certitude in which our souls at last find rest. *Amen.*

DUNCAN HOWLETT, *The First Church of Boston* (*Unitarian*)

BIBLIOGRAPHY

TOWARD A REPRESENTATIVE BIBLIOGRAPHY

This fraction of the good books on prayer and of prayers is one starting-point toward broadening and deepening our knowledge of prayer and the channel in us leading to the patiently waiting God.

A. The Devotional Approach

TERTULLIAN, Q. S. F.: *Concerning Prayer and Concerning Baptism*. London: Macmillan, 1919
The first treatise on Christian prayer.

FOSDICK, HARRY EMERSON: *The Meaning of Prayer*. New York: Association Press, 1915
Still one of the most helpful devotional approaches to the subject.

CLAUDEL, PAUL: *Lord, Teach Us to Pray*, tr. by Ruth Bethell. New York: Longmans, 1948
The devotional life in fresh light, by a French poet.

B. Studies for the General Reader

JONES, RUFUS M.: *The Double Search*. New York: Winston, 1906
Penetrating insights by this great mystical Quaker

PUGLISI PICO, MARIO: *Prayer*. New York: Macmillan, 1929
Toward an historical philosophy of prayer.

STEERE, DOUGLAS V.: *Prayer and Worship*. New York: Association Press, 1938
One of the Hazen Books on Religion. A skillful handling in brief compass, blending wit and wisdom.

BUTTRICK, GEORGE A.: *Prayer*. New York: Abingdon-Cokesbury Press, 1942
A big book on the whole subject, full of helpful wisdom.

HARKNESS, GEORGIA: *Prayer and the Common Life*. New York: Abingdon-Cokesbury Press, 1948
A broad view, sound thought, in simple, suggestive treatment.

STEPHENS, JOHN UNDERWOOD: *A Simple Guide to Prayer*. New York: Abingdon, 1957

A book for beginning or enlarging prayer experience, in a prose whose poetic overtones are very suggestive and helpful.

C. THEOLOGICAL AND DETAILED STUDIES

HASTINGS, JAMES: *Prayer*. In the *Great Christian Doctrines Series*. New York: Scribners, 1915

Reverent and scholarly, a "standard" in its field.

STREETER, B. H., *et al: Concerning Prayer*. London: Macmillan, 1916

Also for those who would drink deep but safely.

LILLEY, ALFRED L.: *Prayer in Christian Theology*. London: Student Christian Movement, 1925

A valuable doctrinal history: brief but suggestive.

HEILER, FRIEDRICH: *Prayer*. London: Oxford, 1932

A translation of *Das Gebet*, the renowned study of the history and psychology of prayer in all religions.

GOSSIP, ARTHUR J.: *In the Secret Place of the Most High*. New York: Scribners, 1947

How to pray; serious, capable work, skillful use of good quotations.

JONES, ILION T.: *A Historical Approach to Evangelical Worship*. New York: Abingdon, 1954

Some history here of the pastoral prayer, with Calvin's fervent warning against it, to begin with, still pertinent.

D. COLLECTIONS OF PRAYERS

1. Compilations for Churches

The Psalter and the Lord's Prayer can never be omitted or taken for granted in such a list as this.

The Book of Common Prayer.

Editions by Cambridge Univ. Press, Harpers, Morehouse-Gorham, Nelson, Oxford Univ. Press, Seabury Press.

After the Bible, the starting-point for all English-speaking students of prayers.

A Book of Worship for Free Churches. New York: Oxford: 1948

Here the Congregationalists return, in prodigal-son fashion, to the spirit (and some of the letters) of the above title. A splendid work of many hands for many occasions.

2. Prayers by Noted Poets

Prayers of John Donne, selected and edited with an essay on Donne's idea of prayer, by Herbert Umbach. New York: Bookman Associates, 1951

STEVENSON, ROBERT LOUIS: *Prayers Written at Vailima*. New York: Scribners, 1908

ROSSETTI, CHRISTINA: *Annus Domini* (1874), and *The Face of the Deep* (1892)

These are prose works not mainly about prayer.

SAMUEL JOHNSON: *Dr. Johnson's Prayers*, edited by D. Elton Trueblood, with an essay on his religion. New York: Harpers, 1947

3. Anthologies

TILESTON, MARY W.: *Prayers Ancient and Modern*. Boston: Little, Brown, 1900

A prayer a day, from the two-thousand-year treasury.

FOX, SELINA F.: *A Chain of Prayer Across the Ages,* New York, Dutton. Revised Edit., 1943

NOYES, MORGAN PHELPS: *Prayers for Services*. New York: Scribners, 1934

ALDRICH, DONALD B., ed.: *The Golden Book of Prayer*. New York: Dodd-Mead, 1941

Excellent in choices, prefaces, organization and format.

McCAULEY, LEON and ELFRIEDA: *The Book of Prayers*. New York: A Dell First Edition, 1954

Drs. Anderson, Scherer, Buttrick, Sockman, and Suter advised on this extremely practical and lifting volume with an introduction by Harry Emerson Fosdick.

4. Books of Prayers by Single Authors

HUNTER, JOHN: *Devotional Services*. New York: Dutton, 1901

NEWTON, JOSEPH FORT: *Altar Stairs*. New York: Macmillan, 1928

SCHMIECHEN, SAMUEL S: *Pastoral Prayers for the Church Year*. New York: Abingdon, 1957.

SUTER, JOHN W.: *Prayers of the Spirit*. New York: Harpers, 1943

STEPHENS, JOHN UNDERWOOD: *Prayers of the Christian Life*. New York: Oxford, 1952

MARSHALL, CATHERINE, ed.: *Prayers of Peter Marshall*. New York: Mc-Graw-Hill, 1954

5. Books of Special Prayers by Single Authors

TITTLE, ERNEST FREMONT: *A Book of Pastoral Prayers*. New York: Abingdon-Cokesbury, 1951

This volume (with a pertinent essay on the pastoral prayer) together with Henry Ward Beecher's *Prayers from Plymouth Pulpit*, 1867, and two anonymous "Pulpit Prayers by Eminent Preachers," one English, one American, both turn-of-the-century, are about all such volumes we have until the present work in the field of collected pastoral prayers.

RAUSCHENBUSCH, WALTER: *Prayers of Social Awakening.* Boston: Pilgrim Press, 1909

Prototypes of today's particularized prayers by the sweet singer of the social gospel.

BARTLETT, ROBERT M.: *A Boy's Book of Prayers.* Boston: Pilgrim Press, 1930

SLATTERY, MARGARET: *A Girl's Book of Prayers.* Boston: Pilgrim Press, 1942

DICKS, RUSSELL L., *ed.: Comfort Ye My People.* New York: Macmillan, 1947

SPERRY, WILLARD L., *ed.: Prayers for Private Devotion in Wartime.* New York: Harpers, 1943

The British Broadcasting Company: *New Every Morning,* the Prayer book of the Daily Broadcast. London: 1936

INDICES

1. INDEX OF SUBJECTS

II. INDEX OF CONTRIBUTORS

FOR ADDITIONAL PRAYERS